# MATTERS OF
# BELONGING

Sidestone Press

# MATTERS OF BELONGING

## Ethnographic Museums in a Changing Europe

Wayne Modest, Nicholas Thomas,
Doris Prlić & Claudia Augustat (eds)

© 2019 Individual authors

Published by Sidestone Press, Leiden
www.sidestone.com

Lay-out & cover design: Sidestone Press
Photograph cover: Pixolar Photography (Lara Eva Tompa)
  The photograph documents the performance of artist Alana Jelinek's work *Europe the Game* during the SWICH conference at the Research Center for Material Culture, Leiden, November 2016.

ISBN 978-90-8890-777-7 (softcover)
ISBN 978-90-8890-778-4 (hardcover)
ISBN 978-90-8890-779-1 (PDF e-book)

# Contents

Acknowledgements     7

Introduction: Ethnographic Museums and     9
the Double Bind
    Wayne Modest

## HERITAGE     23

1. The Museum Inside-out: Twenty Observations     25
    Nicholas Thomas

2. *Museums and Source Communities*: Reflections     37
and Implications
    Laura Peers

3. Collaboration and the Dilemma of the Exotic: A Research Note     55
    Barbara Plankensteiner

4. Our House Is Made of Thin, Burning Ice. Let's Dance     69
    Sandra Ferracuti

## CREATIVITY     87

5. Questions of Belonging     89
    Alana Jelinek

6. Love and Loss in the Ethnographic Museum     101
    Rajkamal Kahlon

7. Eyes in the Back of Your Head: A Talisman Against     111
Disillusionment
    Bianca Baldi

8. I Came as a Stranger     123
    Aleksandra Pawloff

9. The Long Walk: Following the Tick-Ticking     135
Sounds into the Unknown – or, The Omitted
    Jacqueline Hoàng Nguyễn

# INCLUSION 147

**10. Shared Authority Matters: Collaboration with Heritage Bearers with Migrant Background** 149

Tina Palaić and Bojana Rogelj Škafar

**11. Uncomfortable Memory and Community Participation at the Barcelona Ethnological and World Cultures Museum** 165

Salvador García Arnillas and
Lluís-Josep Ramoneda Aigüadé

**12. *The Making of a Point of View*: A Participatory Exhibition at the Pigorini Museum in Rome** 177

Rosa Anna Di Lella and Loretta Paderni

**13. Out of Boxes: Touching wor(l)ds moving pictures A Collective Case Study on a Collaborative Exhibition at the Weltmuseum Wien, Vienna.** 193

UrbanNomadMixes

**14. For Contingent Collaboration: The Making of the *Afterlives of Slavery* Exhibition at the Tropenmuseum** 207

Rita Ouédraogo, Robin Lelijveld, Martin Berger,
Richard Kofi, and Wayne Modest

**Biographies of Contributors** 219

# Acknowledgements

Acknowledging the contribution of the many people who read, critiqued, influenced or otherwise contributed to any book is an important part of the publication process. In our case, the collaborative spirit of the project from which this publication emerges, like the publication itself, makes acknowledging those who contributed not just courteous, but obvious, even vital.

This publication is an outcome of the four-year collaborative project *Sharing a World of Inclusion, Creativity and Heritage* (SWICH), which was co-funded by the Creative Europe Programme of the European Union. SWICH, like the earlier, similar collaborative projects before it, was conceived to enable ethnographic and world cultures museums across Europe to develop more inclusive and decolonial practices together with diverse stakeholders.

We would like to thank all of these stakeholders. All the artists involved in the project, and the other critical friends, whose ongoing questioning of the histories, ethics and continued relevance of these institutions continue to challenge those who work in them to develop better, more inclusive and just practices. The project partners, the colleagues at the ten partner museums, and the many participants of conferences, lab meetings and workshops: together we have engaged in numerous discussions that have challenged taken-for-granted assumptions in our ways of working. We have also experimented with new practices, tested them, and critiqued them together.

This publication would not have been possible without the support of Sidestone Press and especially Corné van Woerdekom for their support in the process of production and publication. And, the support from the Creative Europe programme of the European Union was also indispensable throughout the project.

At the core of this book's ambitions is to push more creative and rigorous practices of collaboration. We hope that the contributors have found the process of creating this volume rewarding and part of fulfilling this ambition. We want to thank you for your efforts. We hope that our readers will see this publication as representative of an ongoing commitment by numerous people, including activists, community representatives and museum professionals, to developing new tools and more innovative and inclusive practices that will help us reshape ethnographic and world cultures museums to become more critical sites from which to undo colonialism's lasting hold. Such a commitment must include practices of solidarity and a shared belief in more just futures. We hope this publication, like the project from which it emerged, is one step in this direction.

# Introduction: Ethnographic Museums and the Double Bind

WAYNE MODEST

Amidst the 'anxious politics' (Modest and de Koning 2016) that animates discussions about the present and future of Europe, battles over citizenship and belonging – over who is considered to be or who can be European – have also been battles over European heritage. Cultural studies theorist Stuart Hall brought this to our attention in the late 1990s. In his 'Whose Heritage? Un-settling "The Heritage", Reimagining the Post-Nation', he asks: 'Who is the Heritage *for*?' He continues to argue that, 'In the British case the answer is clear. It is intended for those who "belong" – a society which is imagined as, in broad terms, culturally homogeneous and unified' (Hall 1999, 6). A similar claim could be made about other parts of Europe today. And it is in response to such claims that the authors in this book, like the diverse cases which they describe, respond.

Indeed, imaginings of European belonging as homogenous, both culturally and racially, have only intensified, manifesting in growing right-wing, exclusionary political formations, and characterised by increased forms of xenophobic and Islamophobic nationalism. Some scholars have discussed this as the 'culturalisation of citizenship' (Duyvendak et al. 2016). These forms of imagining the nation presume that the multicultural political project – that pluralising polity we have come to know across Europe, which Hall identifies as having started in earnest in the aftermath of WWII – has failed. Formerly colonised peoples and labour migrants now living in Europe are imagined as a threat to European identity, to its culture, to its housing stock, and to its welfare provisions (Bhambra, 2009; de Koning and Modest 2017). It is they, according to such arguments, that do not belonging. Hall (1999, 6) declares: 'It is long past time to radically question this foundational assumption'.

Hall's call to us is not simply to rethink the concept of heritage, but to rethink our understanding of what the heritage of a changed, postcolonial Europe is, or could be. This would demand a radical questioning of who constitutes the subject to whom European heritage *belongs*. If British, indeed if European, heritage, was in the past taken as belonging to, or reflective of, a distinct and culturally homogenous group of people, then in the postcolonial moment, with the increased migration of people from former European colonies and other parts of the world, questions of European heritage and belonging must include them in the mix. *Matters of Belonging* takes up Hall's challenge through the lens of ethnographic and world cultures museums.

Within Europe, ethnography and world cultures museums occupy a unique position, their formation closely bound up with the very ways that Europe has come to define itself in relation to other parts of the world, to its *Others* outside. Numerous scholars have explored the emergence and development of these museums alongside Europe's colonial endeavours, and how they in many ways bolstered colonialism. Tony Bennett (1995), for example, has shown how museums were part of an assemblage of governmental technologies, that included World Fairs, involved in the training of good civic behaviour, the governing of civic conduct. His ongoing work on museums has also been concerned with how these museums participated in fashioning a hierarchy of humankind; the ordering, classifying and governing of colonised subjects; and the relationship of these museums with the development of scientific disciplines associated with colonialism (2004). Bennett's writings form part of a now voluminous body of critical work that takes the ethnographic museums as one of the visible signs – if not the most visible within the museum landscape – of colonial afterlives in the present, a node where colonial hierarchies, extractive economies and violence materialise and cluster. I have argued elsewhere that to see ethnographic museums as occupying such a 'privileged' position for colonial entailments is to miss the widely distributed nature of colonial afterlives in the present, which may only serve to limit our ability to effectively address them.[1] However, it does remind us of the positioning of such museums as central spaces for the reworking or working through of our postcolonial present, and the fashioning of other futures.

Other scholars such as Glenn Penny have also contributed to this work to unpack the complex entanglement between museums, colonialism and, for example, the development of modern scientific disciplines such as anthropology (ethnology) or archaeology. Writing on the important role that ethnographic museums played in the growth of German ethnology in the nineteenth century, Penny (2002) argues that while scientific and collecting practices have been seen to be in the service of, and dependent on, the networks and structures of colonialism, this, at least within the German context, cannot be reduced singularly to imperial aspirations, or to legitimising racial science. Rather, he makes the case for us to see these efforts as infused with larger cosmopolitan ideals, informed by an interest in developing theories of humanity. While I would question whether this is a distinction that can be made so easily, choosing one side or the other, Penny's work has been an important part of exploring the entangled histories in which ethnographic museums have participated. Other scholars like Stocking (1988) and Conn (1998), have similarly explored the relationship between the development of museums, colonialism and different forms of knowledge.

These early studies have undoubtedly been important to the field. Coming at the same time as a rise in broader museum studies critique, the so-called New Museology (see, for example, Vergo 1997), they offered more grounded exploration of institutional and collections histories in relation to rising postcolonial critique of museums.

A similarly influential body of literature also emerged that examined the larger representational economy of which these museums were part, critiquing how they positioned former colonised peoples as temporally and hierarchically other to

---

[1] I have presented this as part of several presentations on ethnographic museums and their futures.

the West, even as these museums tried to understand the plurality of human life[2]. James Clifford (1997), for example, has explored how museums participated in an art/culture system that helped to forge categories of art and ethnography, tied to notions of the West and its Others, and represented in the hierarchies of objects as they find their way into different types of museums, often influenced by the art market. Clifford's work has, however, also been important for us reimagining how these museums have themselves functioned as 'contact zones', prioritising the voice of indigenous communities in museum representational practices. This interest in practices of representation would only grow, leading to a spate of publications. For example, the seminal series published by the Smithsonian Publishers and edited by Ivan Karp et al., which includes *Exhibiting Cultures: The Poetics and Politics of Museum Display* (1991), *Museum and Communities: The Politics of Public Culture* (1992) and *Museum Frictions: Public Cultures Global Transformations* (2006), locates the museums within a larger field of contestation about representation within local and global contexts. Peers and Brown's *Museums and Source Communities* (2003), about which Laura Peers reflects in chapter two of this publication, also falls within this line of scholarship.

While some of the earlier works mentioned were more historical and focussed on museum collecting and representational practices in relation to the nexus of colonial knowledge and power, the latter studies have been more concerned with issues related to the practices of representation within the postcolonial moment. In his chapter in this volume, Nicholas Thomas reflects on some of the issues raised by such criticism and where he considers these to fall short.

Of course, critiques of the practices of ethnographic and world cultures museums have not only come from academic circles, but also from diverse activists and members of stakeholder communities. There is already a long tradition of activism from indigenous peoples around practices of representation within ethnographic museums. Currently, there is a growing transnational activism demanding the decolonisation of the museum. Several scholars have also addressed these issues (Golding and Modest 2014; Onciul 2015).

This brief account of these histories of critique is not to elide their importance; we believe that such critiques have been and remain valid and urgent for the shifts that have occurred in ethnographic and world cultures museums in recent years. We take these histories and critique as given, as foundational to our concerns, rather than rehearse them once more. Indeed, what we propose is that it may be precisely these entangled relations with the colonial past – of extraction and violence, of appropriation and misrepresentation – that recommend these institutions as powerful sites for thinking through colonial entailments in the present.

---

2   See, for example, Shatanawi (2009). Several of the authors arguing this position draw on Johannes Fabian's now classic *Time and the Other: How anthropology makes its object.*

Contrary to the now famous and oft-repeated statement made several decades ago by black feminist activist and scholar Audre Lorde (1983), it may precisely be with the master's tools that we can do the work of dismantling the master's house. Of ethnographic museums we can ask how we might think other futures out of the irreparable evil[3] that colonialism represents. And, moreover, how these museums might help us rethink European futures as more equitable. The authors here draw on a history of practice developed within these institutions to address some of the most urgent critiques of the institutions themselves, locating them within the anxious political discourse about European futures after colonialism.

## The Double Bind of Critique and Recognition

If discussions about the present and future of Europe are discussions about who is European or what constitutes European heritage, then ethnographic and world cultures museums occupy a contradictory position in these discussions, what we could call a 'double bind'. On the one hand, these museums are prominent fulcrums on which critiques of colonial durabilities have focussed, in which they may represent signs of colonial times and perhaps even perceived as scenes of colonial crimes (Stoler 2019). Such critiques have been made in relation to questions surrounding the ownership of the collections these museums now hold, the elision of the colonial genealogies of their own formation; and the (mis)representation of formerly colonised peoples. These aspects of the museum's work have correctly been subject to a long and sustained critique, one that started several decades ago, some of which we have already mentioned.

Almost contradictorily, however, these museums have been imagined, indeed mobilised, as institutions with a central role to play in connecting with diverse postcolonial and post-migrant communities within European changing polities, as spaces of recognition or sites for *belonging work*. This is precisely what we want to explore in more detail here. Bennett (2006) describes museums as 'differencing machines', not so much in their earlier role of fashioning difference, but more in the work they do in connecting with global multicultural formations that now characterise our present moment. Similarly, Paul Basu (2011) invites us to think about how museum objects may connect in complex ways with diasporic subjects in their negotiation of issues of identity and belonging, and how they may *remit* value from European centres to the cultures and countries from where objects came. Such recognition work has also been the prerogative of ethnographic museums.

---

3   We refer to irreparable evil here drawing on the recent work of David Scott presented at the Research Center for Material Culture on 1 November 2018 (https://www.materialculture.nl/en/events/new-world-slavery-irreparable-evil).

Following the argument of Mary Stevens (2007) for museums in general, ethnographic and world cultures museums have become *authorities of recognition.* For Stevens this happens in three senses: ´as a devolved agency of the state, [they] are seen as conferring legitimacy'; they provide 'a relatively neutral space for the negotiation of competing claims'; and 'within the museum, groups position themselves in relation not only to each other but also with regard to multiple heritages; the possibility for both spatial and temporal positioning...' (Stevens 2007, 32). We suggest similar practices for ethnographic and world cultures museums.

Stevens' study of museums as spaces of recognition draws on scholars working on holocaust memory (Feuchtwang 2003, for example), where recognition is tied to 'a demand for acknowledgement of a grievous loss', which he suggests 'is often a grievance described and treated in terms very like that of debt, something which needs redemption' (Stevens 2007, 32, quoting Feuchtwang 2003, 77). Perhaps the work of recognition for ethnographic and world cultures museums, entangled as they have been with Europe's colonial project, may well be one of redemption for historical injustice, like taking up the master's tools. Such is the suggestion of many of the authors assembled here in how they have explored the work and potential of these museums.

This publication brings questions of belonging together with issues related to the redemptive work that museums can do to address historical injustices. It addresses the double bind of critique and recognition by exploring diverse models that these museums have been developing over the years to address the colonial entailments in the present. The chapters converge on a particular claim, one that we admit may be too hopeful: ethnographic and world cultures museums, even though they may fall short of their own radical imaginings, are developing practices that address entrenched colonial afterlives in the world today. Being attentive to these practices and pushing them to their limits may reshape museum work in ways that are committed to more inclusive and more equitable futures. The double bind, then, may open these museums up as important sites where such work may happen.

The book is, however, not celebratory or congratulatory of a triumphal overcoming by ethnographic museums of their troubled pasts. Rather its aim is to think critically about these museums' responses to longstanding critique, both pitfalls as well as positives, to sketch out possible futures for museums generally, and ethnographic museums specifically, as they try to locate themselves within discussions about Europe and its futures.

## Sharing a World of Inclusion, Creativity, and Heritage

The book and many of the case studies presented here emerge from the Sharing a World of Inclusion, Creativity and Heritage (SWICH) project, co-funded by Creative Europe Programme of the European Union, which places ethnographic museums at the centre of debates about Europe's shifting polity, heritage, citizenship, and belonging. SWICH was the most recent incarnation of a series of collaborative network and research projects among ethnographic museums across Europe, which includes the previous projects, the International Network of Ethnographic Museums (RIME) and the European Network of Diasporas Associations and Ethnographic Museums (READ-ME). Coming together across diverse political climates and citizenship regimes, legal frameworks, and colonial/migratory histories, these projects have questioned the role of ethnographic and world cultures museums in debates on how to define Europe, the European, and European heritage. Grappling with these questions, the authors here focus on the relationships developed between the museum and diverse stakeholders, especially artists and different community members.

## Matters of Belonging

This volume brings together academics, curators, artists, and activists to think both about *matter* – things in museum collections – and why, how, and for whom they matter. At the same time, it is about *belonging* – in the double sense of the word: possession (this thing belongs to me) and feeling a part of something bigger (I belong to a community). The book comes at an important moment in the global heritage landscape, as questions of who owns cultural property are arguably more prevalent than ever[4]. While we do not address issues of provenance and return here, at least not directly, we do explore the meaning that objects have or may have for diverse stakeholders within national and global contexts.

In her chapter in this volume, Laura Peers reflects on her 2003 seminal publication (co-edited with Alison Brown) about museums and source communities, in which they explored redemptive or reparative practices within museums, bringing objects together with communities of origin. As Peers [this publication] writes, *Museums and Source Communities: A Routledge Reader* was driven by 'a sense of frustration arising from the disconnect between the extraordinary historic collec-

---

4   I refer here to recent discussions across Europe about the return of objects acquired during the colonial period, which has resulted in a flurry of provenance research projects in museums, especially in Germany. The recent report by Felwine Sarr and Benedicte Savoy (http://restitutionreport2018.com/sarr_savoy_en.pdf) on objects from Africa in French museum collections is especially important here.

tions from North American Indigenous communities in British museums and those communities themselves'.

Her chapter in this volume is important not only for re-emphasising the important work that museums can do to bring communities together with historical collections, for cultural resilience and the revitalisation of artistic or ritual practices, but also for tracing the genealogy of our engagement with the concept of source community. Numerous authors may have taken issue with the concept of source community, as a term or even as a practice (see, for example, Boast 2011); we cannot, however, deny its force as a model aimed at developing more inclusive, even reparative practices. Peers' longstanding work within the museum field has evidenced such practices.

While the issue of matter as possession runs through this publication, our main concern is with the concept of belonging as feeling a part of something – indeed, with belonging as citizenship. This question has spurred much writing in museum studies focussed on social inclusion and diversity. We hope to complement such writings with examples of grounded, ethnographic case studies of how belonging works. As notions of belonging are often still racialised or culturalised, especially in our current political moment in Europe, we argue that ethnographic and world cultures museums are especially important sites through which to address how belonging matters today.

## The Book

The book is organised in three sections, according to the main thematic divisions of the SWICH project. Section one addresses the idea of heritage in the broadest sense, with chapters that explore the complex entanglements of colonial afterlives/heritage in the present, the museum as a site of heritage with its own legacy of collecting and presentation, as well as objects as heritage. These chapters locate their concerns within discussions about belonging in and to Europe today. At stake for the authors is not just ownership in relation to objects' potential return, but claims to such heritage – to access them or collaborate in their interpretation – that diverse individuals or communities may make, as citizens, be they postcolonial or (post) migrants. Barbara Plankensteiner, for example, addresses the difficult issue of what happens when so-called communities living in Europe mobilise essentialising tropes in festivals or other performance traditions, within the context of museums that have long been critiqued for such practices. She shows how such strategic deployment of traditions, practiced across Europe with the support of local embassies and community groups, are organised to celebrate, even self-represent positive aspects of, 'culture' or 'identity' that can counter negative stereotypes or practices of marginalisation. Plankensteiner's article does not proffer solutions for such practices, but rather invites more scholarly attention for them.

Ferracuti, in her exploration of a platform of immigrants of African descent living in Stuttgart, with whom she collaborates to develop the new permanent exhibition at the Linden-Museum Stuttgart, asks how the representation of transnational notions of belonging in museums might help to dislodge reductive ideas of national bounded cultures, or combat stereotypical notions of Africa and 'African culture' circulating across Europe. Ferracuti locates herself in the discussion, as an immigrant from Italy now living in Germany, not to suggest that all migrant belongings are the same, but to show how allegiances might be thought about differently within transnational contexts. She points to the role that ethnographic museums can play in decentring our philosophy of the world and inviting us to rethink our common responsibility for repairing past wrongs. Nicholas Thomas, in a reflective essay, cautions us to be mindful that postcolonial and cultural studies critique of museums, which he identifies as emergent over the last few decades, does not only serve to dismiss the deeply grounded and important work of curators and other scholars within these museums, but can be taken as opportunities to strengthen these practices and develop even more suitable museum methodologies to address issues of the present. Thomas continues the work he started in a recent publication (2016) of reimagining the immense potential that these museums, with their deep and complex collections, can play as sites for reimagining other, better futures. This publication is already a step in this direction.

Section two, which we think offers the greatest innovation for the field, focusses on the work of contemporary artists who have been involved in longstanding critical engagements with ethnographic museums and their practices. Our contention is that despite the growing tradition of inviting contemporary artists in to address the challenges and limitations of ethnographic and world cultures museums, very little has been published on the work that they have done. This publication invited five contemporary artists who have recently worked with ethnographic museums to reflect on such efforts. All of the artists were invited by different museums in the SWICH project to work within their archives, with their histories and their practices, not just to critique but also to imagine, together with staff, new modes of engaging these (colonial) archives in the present. In their chapters, that weave text together with their artwork, they reflect on their complex positionality within museums that often regard them as *the other within*. Their articles demonstrate ways in which these museums interpolate specifically positioned subjects in affective ways, as colonial structures continue to live on in the present. The publication of these five artists' essays serve to complement another publication of the SWICH artists in residence programme (Noack and de Castro, 2018).

Rajkamal Kahlon, who was the artist in residence at the Weltmuseum Wien, examines how forms of embodied, radical empathy can help to recover the lives of those that colonial violence has made invisible. She likens ethnographic museums with holocaust museums, as sites of memory and commemoration for those who have endured another serious historical atrocity – that of colonialism. At the same time, Kahlon's open, even ambiguous, use of the term holocaust implicates these museums in this same act of historical injustice. Jacqueline Hoàng Nguyễn, working at the ethnographic museum in Stockholm, raises the question of how such institutions, 'which have long been central to the construction of racial categories, remain unable, even unwilling, to name and confront the very legacy they have helped to create'. Alana Jelinek, who has worked for a long time with the Museum of Archaeology and Anthropology at Cambridge, traces her genealogy as an artist, and her own longstanding engagement with ethnographic museums, to explore the double meaning of the term belonging, as possession and as a feeling of being a part of something. Jelinek reminds us of the longer genealogy of artists' critical intervention in museums, locating her own work within earlier work such as Fred Wilson's critical *Mining the Museum* project of 1992 at the Maryland Historical Society.

All these artists present the personal, ambiguous engagement, a relation characterised by discomfort or friction, that many contemporary artists, indeed many (postcolonial or post-migrant) citizens may have with ethnographic museums. Unlike some, however, these five artists worked within these museums, within the *belly of the beast* as Stuart Hall would say, to imagine them anew, from inside.

Focussed on specific participatory projects carried out by museums, the chapters in the last section *Inclusion* address some of the concerns for museums working with communities across Europe. These essays are grounded in specific historic and national contexts, in specific collection histories and specific case studies. Beyond practical issues, for example, of time or money available for projects, what are some of the challenges to doing community work within museums amidst the anxious politics of present-day Europe? Do specific ideas about 'who is a citizen' make it difficult to engage with certain communities, or even to use the concept of community itself (as it is, for example, in France)[5]? How does the current political moment limit or allow for doing community work within a particular country or city? How do histories of migration, or of colonialism or imperialism, affect how this work can be done? And how do intersectional categories – gender, sexual orientation, racial-ethnic identity, class, etc. – inform such work?

Reading the chapters about Barcelona and Rome together, we are prompted to think critically about how colonialism is elided in many contemporary discussions about Europe's past, present, and future. García Arnillas and Ramoneda Aigüadé note that their attempts to address the colonial past through museum collections was done within a national context that *forgot* this history, including in the educa-

---

5   Throughout the SWICH project our French colleagues reminded us of the difficulty with using the concept of community within a French political context. If, as they reminded us, everyone is a citizen of the republic then distinguishing people by communities is not a common (even a discouraged) practice in France.

tional curriculum. Their article also raised questions about their own practice. In their efforts to address the invisiblised colonial history through inclusive and participatory practices at the Ethnological and World Cultures Museum in Barcelona, they left the figure of the curator underrepresented in the exhibition's narrative designed to share authority, arguably reproducing a long-established trope of invisible curatorial authority. This does not, however, limit the importance of the work done to address Spain's colonial past in the museum. In contrast, in both Rome and Vienna, the voices of the curators were much more present. Indeed, as Camilo Antonio points out, we may better rethink categories and diaspora identities if we squarely place curators into the mix of players whose belonging needs to be questioned [a similar strategy was also discussed by Ferracuti].

The museums in both Vienna and Rome, as discussed by Antonio, and Di Lella and Paderni, respectively, brought diasporas of objects together with people from diasporic communities. In both cases there was a tension between the individual meaning of objects and the meanings ascribed to the objects by the museum. They echo Nicholas Thomas' contribution here, who also questions such practices. Such questions surrounding diaspora, museums and collections have also been taken up by scholars such as Paul Basu (2017), who suggests the need for more attentiveness to the diasporic condition as a more unstable, messy and in-between space, indeed as a space of the political that is not easily reducible to one thing or another, but is a contingent category[6].

Ethnographic museums, their collections, and their histories, cannot be too easily reduced to the diasporas living in Europe. Nor can these collections and museums bracket the political concerns of those people living in Europe today. Of course, nineteenth-century collections cannot be required to speak to the same politics then and now. Yet, gestures towards thinking the two diasporas together, and towards thinking about objects and originating communities, may still be urgent, even if only to come to better understandings of the complexity of transnational belonging, in people and in objects [see Ferracuti, this volume]. And thinking about diaspora here – as opposed to people over there – may in fact be a false division in a globalised heritage world. The borders of heritage are not simply national, especially if we agree that the distribution of heritage resources globally reflect other unequal global distributions of resources. As part of international diplomacy, ethnographic collections also play an important role, even if it remains understudied. Plankensteiner alludes to this in her chapter, where she shows how art practices in Vienna form part of a politics of rights claims for indigenous peoples living in Brazil.

---

[6] For other critical engagement with diaspora see Hall (2000) and Clifford (1994).

These are the concerns that this publication addresses. They are addressed from inside the museum, by curators, artists, activists and academics engaging with academic and popular/public critique. In some cases, these are very personal reflections. Nonetheless, we hope the reader will take this volume as a modest attempt that accepts the fraught histories of ethnographic and world cultures museums, not as something to push against but to confront, indeed a past that we must mobilise, must be understood, in our efforts to fashion more equitable and just non-imperial futures.

## References

Basu, Paul. 2011. 'Object Diasporas, Resourcing Communities: Sierra Leonean Collections in the Global Museumscape'. *Museum Anthropology* 34, no. 1: 28-42.

Basu, Paul, ed. 2017. *The Inbetweenness of Things: Materializing Mediation and Movement Between Worlds*. London: Bloomsbury Publishing.

Bennett, Tony. 1995. *The Birth of the Museum: History, Theory, Politics*. London: Routledge.

Bennett, Tony. 2004. *Pasts Beyond Memory: Evolution, Museums, Colonialism*. London: Routledge.

Bennett, Tony. 2006. 'Exhibition, Difference and the Logic of Culture'. In *Museum Frictions: Public Cultures/Global Transformations*, edited by I. Karp and C. Kratz, 46-69. Durham: Durham University Press.

Bhambra, Gurminder K. 2009. 'Postcolonial Europe, or Understanding Europe in Times of the Postcolonial'. In *The SAGE Handbook of European Studies*, edited by Chris Rumford, 69-85. London: SAGE Publications Ltd.

Boast, Robin. 2011. 'Neocolonial Collaboration: Museum as Contact Zone Revisited'. *Museum Anthropology* 34, no. 1: 56-70.

Clifford, James. 1994. 'Diasporas'. *Cultural Anthropology* 9, no. 3: 302-338.

Clifford, James. 1997. *Routes: Travel and Translation in the Late Twentieth Century*. Cambridge, MA: Harvard University Press.

Conn, Steven. 1998. *Museums and American Intellectual Life, 1876-1926*. Chicago: University of Chicago Press.

Duyvendak, Jan Willem, Peter Geschiere, and Evelien Tonkens, eds. 2016. *The Culturalization of Citizenship: Belonging and Polarization in a Globalizing World*. London: Palgrave Macmillan.

Fabian, Johannes. 2014. *Time and the Other: How Anthropology Makes Its Object*. New York: Columbia University Press.

Feuchtwang, S. 2003. 'Loss: Transmissions, Recognitions, Authorisations'. In *Regimes of Memory*, edited by S. Radstone and K. Hodgkin, 76-89. London: Routledge.

Golding, Vivian, and Wayne Modest, eds. 2013. *Museums and Communities: Curators, Collections and Collaboration.* London: Bloomsbury.

Hall, Stuart. 1999. 'Whose Heritage? Un-settling "The Heritage", Re-imagining the Post-Nation'. *Third Text* 13, no. 49: 3-13.

Hall, Stuart. 2000. 'Cultural Identity and Diaspora'. In *Diaspora and Visual Culture*, edited by Nicholas Mirzeoff, 35-47. London: Routledge.

Karp, I. et al., eds. 2006. *Museum Frictions: Public Cultures/Global Transformations.* Durham: Durham University Press.

Karp, Ivan, Christine Kreamer, and Steven D. Lavine, eds. 1992. *Museums and Communities: The Politics of Public Culture.* Washington, DC: Smithsonian Institution Press.

Koning, A., and W. Modest. 2017. 'Anxious Politics in Postcolonial Europe'. *American Anthropologist* 119, no. 3: 524-526.

Lorde, Audre. 1983. 'The Master's Tools Will Never Dismantle the Master's House'. In *This Bridge Called My Back: Writings by Radical Women of Color,* edited by Cherríe Moraga and Gloria Anzaldúa, 98-101. New York: Kitchen Table.

Modest, Wayne, and Anouk de Koning. 2016. 'Anxious Politics in the European City: An Introduction'. *Patterns of Prejudice* 50: 97-108.

Noack, Georg, and Inés de Castro, eds. 2018. *Co-Creation Labs: Illuminating Guests, Artists and New Voices in European Museums of World Culture.* Dresden: Sandstein Verlag.

Onciul, Bryony. 2015. *Museums, Heritage and Indigenous Voice: Decolonizing Engagement.* London: Routledge.

Penny, H. Glenn. 2002. *Objects of Culture: Ethnology and Ethnographic Museums in Imperial Germany.* Chapel Hill, NC: Univ. of North Carolina Press.

Sarr, Felwine, and Benedicte Savoy. 2018. *The Restitution of African Cultural Heritage. Toward a New Relational Ethics.* http://restitutionreport2018.com/sarr_savoy_en.pdf.

Shatanawi, M. 2009. 'Contemporary Art in Ethnographic Museums'. In *The Global Art World: Audiences, Markets, and Museums,* edited by H. Belting and A. Buddensieg, 368-384. OstfildernRuit: Hatje Cantz.

Stoler, Ann Laura. 2019. *Scenes of a Crime: Ethnological Museums in the Throes of Time.* Unpublished Article.

Stevens, Mary. 2007. 'Museums, Minorities and Recognition: Memories of North Africa in Contemporary France'. *Museum and Society* 5, no. 1: 29-43.

Stocking, George W., ed. 1988. *Objects and Others: Essays on Museums and Material Culture.* Vol. 3. Madison: Univ. of Wisconsin Press.

Thomas, Nicholas. 2016. *The Return of Curiosity: What Museums Are Good for in the 21st Century.* London: Reaktion Books.

Vergo, Peter, ed. 1997. *New Museology.* London: Reaktion Books.

Fig. 1.1. 'Oceania', curated by Peter Brunt and Nicholas Thomas, Royal Academy of Arts, London and Musée du quai Branly-Jacques Chirac, Paris, 2018-19. Photo: Nicholas Thomas.

Heritage

# The Museum Inside-out: Twenty Observations

NICHOLAS THOMAS

Fig. 1.2. 'Kanak: l'art est un parole', curated by Emmanuel Kasarhérou and Roger Boulay, Musée du quai Branly-Jacques Chirac, Paris, 2013-14. Photo: Nicholas Thomas.

1. Over the last three hundred years, European travel, commerce, missionary enterprise, science and colonial governance have brought extensive and extraordinarily varied collections of art and material culture from all parts of the inhabited world to private collections, scientific societies, universities and public museums across Europe, and to similar institutions in some countries elsewhere. The late nineteenth century was notable for an escalation of both anthropological and imperial ambitions, and an intensification of systematic collecting: some expeditions returned with thousands of artefacts, notionally representative of specific cultures and regions.

2. Consequently, not only major national museums but smaller institutions in many regional cities and towns host extensive and complex assemblages of global material culture. These are at once assemblages of precious heritage, resources for diverse cultural projects, and the outcomes and bearers of difficult histories. Certain collections have been deeply studied, authoritatively published and represented through exhibitions in popular museums, while others have been neglected, kept largely in storage, and marginalised in the public cultural sphere and in art worlds that have privileged the European canon.

3. The late twentieth century saw the emergence of new critical discourses, that identified museums as hegemonic knowledge formations and sometimes crudely stigmatized them as illegitimate expressions of elite culture and hierarchy. Museum curators and professionals – among them the authors of critiques in various registers – embraced opportunities to reinvent practice and move toward more collaborative and inclusive ways of working.

4. In the 1990s, some believed museums might be rendered redundant by the proliferation of digital media. Paradoxically, the same period was marked by unprecedented investment. New institutions proliferated internationally, existing museums were extended and renovated, and the museum as a form and an experience was reinvented, embracing ideals of open participation and inclusion.

5. This phase of new and ambitious investment has, however, been nothing if not uneven. While some national institutions have created new conservation and collections facilities, digitised their entire holdings and made them accessible online, and presented exhibitions and temporary projects in engaging and inviting new buildings and precincts, other collections, some of major heritage significance, have been left behind, struggling with limited staff, poor and inaccessible storage and dated and under-visited displays. Just as more accessible and better presented collections generate new interest and strengthen their support base, museums that appear irrelevant, without visible public constituencies, can enter a downward spiral, and may be at risk of closure.

Fig. 1.3. 'Kanak', exhibition view. Photo: Nicholas Thomas.

6. The support of governments and other sponsors for new, renovated and extended museums follows from understanding that they generate a wide range of social benefits: attracting tourists, driving the regeneration of deprived neighbourhoods and regions, fostering social inclusion and enabling the international projection of 'soft' power.

7. While ethnographic museums have long been the 'poor cousins' of prestigious art institutions, they were in fact the first to embrace inclusive and collaborative practices. They recognized responsibilities to engage with the descendants of people who had made the artefacts from which collections were made. Consultative practice developed in fits and starts and the concept of the museum as space of cross-cultural engagement and encounter became axiomatic, and was subsequently embraced by the whole museum sector, from history and science to art institutions: it is now widely affirmed that the museum should be a meeting place, a realm of diversity and dialogue. While the 'contact zone' model may be criticized as a form of co-optation that cannot ameliorate enduring inequalities, practice has not stood still, and arguably advanced from project-specific liaison toward wider and deeper forms of co-production based in enduring relationships, focussed not just on the creation of displays, but now present at the core of the wider range of museum activities – from acquisition projects through conservation and collections management to outreach and social media.

8. The ethnographic museum's engagement with 'source' communities gives such institutions a distinctive and powerful capacity to engage cross-culturally and with minorities in the post-migrant social order that is constitutive of contemporary European nations. No other museums are so profoundly cross-cultural in their formation and none bear the anthropological commitment to engage with and celebrate cultural difference at the core of their history and mission in a comparable way, notwithstanding the longstanding tensions within the discipline between relativist and evolutionist or otherwise hierarchical paradigms, and the discipline's much-debated association or complicity in colonial policy and practice. Yet a history of positive experience in collaborative practice with members of Indigenous communities – typically situated elsewhere in the world – does not necessarily enable work with migrants or their descendants who inhabit neighbourhoods and in many cases suffer deprivation, exclusion and racism in the European cities in which museums are situated. The diversity that ethnographic museums have represented is not the same as the diversity that is most conspicuous around them. There are tensions between Indigenous discourses, in particular the emerging field of Indigenous philosophy, and diaspora-inspired theories and politics. At the same time, museums are addressing

other forms of difference, for example through LGBTQ projects. Being or seeking to be 'all things to all people' is proverbially an expression of weakness or confusion, but is now in effect at the heart of the museum mission, above all for formerly ethnographic institutions now charged with the representation and celebration of world cultures.

9. Across the uneven and heterogeneous museum economy, both the retrenchment of staff in less fortunate institutions and the restructuring of many that are seen as successful have diminished curatorial work, in the double sense that jobs have been lost and curators become, some feel, less influential within their institutions. While it has been positive and necessary that public engagement and learning provision were strengthened, deep knowledge of collections continues to be vital. In so far as it or its status has diminished, institutions are damaged. And this is true especially in ethnographic institutions, because collections are not only typically vast, but also complex in their formation and identity – and hence also in their potential in the present, and their politics – in ways that professionals lacking familiarity and expertise may grasp at best superficially.

10. The humanities and social sciences in recent decades have been transformed by an ascendancy of cultural studies, postmodern and postcolonial theory, associated with fundamentally necessary and fertile critiques of conventional canons and methods. But just recently, political polarisation has rendered critique both cheap and loud, tending to drown out more sustained and careful conversation around historical entanglement and ambiguity. In the particular fields of material culture, the anthropology of art and cross-cultural art history, fine-grained scholarship on local art traditions, artefact genres, the ethnohistories of cultural forms, cross-cultural aesthetics, provenance and the histories of collections has been marginalized by more rhetorical discourse. It is commonly assumed that historical information relevant to collections is readily available online, whereas even for famous or notorious collections such as those associated with the voyages of Captain James Cook, records are widely dispersed, complex and confusing; important material is not digitally available; and much online commentary incorporates misattributions among other forms of misinformation. In general, ethnographic collections are deeply complex material and knowledge formations. Rather like archaeological sites, they are made up of multiple layers and accretions but are also marked by erosion and loss. They cannot be understood without sustained analysis of the material objects themselves, without wide-ranging archival research that must often be comparative, ranging far beyond the institutions and nations in which they may be situated, and would be impoverished without fieldwork and dialogue with Indigenous experts among others, in the communities and regions from which collections derive.

11. Without sustained research, without connoisseurship (in the sense of dedicated material knowledge, not that of art-market savoir-faire), the identities and lives of artefacts and collections are easily misrecognized. A sculpture of an ancestor may be presumed to be, for example, a sacred incarnation, the recipient of ritual offerings, or an artefact that has suffered decontextualization from the religious life of a community, rather than what it may actually be, a replica created for an ethnographer, or an early work of tourist art. These identifications not only inflect the questions of ethics that may be raised about a particular work, but if misrecognized also diminish the opportunity to interpret it in ways salient to narratives of cross-cultural, colonial, global and entangled history.

12. In politics, our time is marked not only by the resurgence of economic nationalism, racism and anti-immigrant populism but also by a revival of oppositional activism on many fronts, from economic inequality to threats to the global environment. In this context, the academic postcolonialism of the 1980s and 1990s has been succeeded by activism toward decolonization, understood precisely not as political event (the independence of countries formerly subject to colonial rule) but as an open-ended emancipatory process, more or less centred upon the acknowledgement of histories of imperial exploitation and violence.

13. It would be surprising if decolonization activists did not target ethnographic museums, but it is notable that their representation of the institutions and their histories is unrelentingly negative. A generation coming to the issues for the first time is largely unaware of the nuances of debate over the last thirty years, and the innovative and critical practice that has followed from it. To the contrary, ethnographic collecting is read as a sort of coda to the colonial project as a totality, as nothing other than one-side appropriation, an extravagantly global expression of greed. There is a crude version of the critique in which museums are defined by colonial theft, and this fact exhausts their meaning: the discourse registers no other identity, activity or social effect in the museum than this, which can only be redressed by the restitution of collections, by implication their total restitution.

14. This stereotypic view is predicated on misrecognition of what museums hold, of the histories of such collections and of the kinds of activity constitutive of the lives of institutions of ethnography and world cultures, in the present and over recent decades. Most artefacts were not stolen but willingly offered in exchange, sometimes as diplomatic gifts, or sold on terms that local vendors considered reasonable, or actively negotiated. To be sure, some artefacts were unambiguously looted, appropriated in the aftermath of punitive raids or similar military actions, and some were bought in contexts where people were in effect coerced, or where

Fig. 1.4. 'Oceania', exhibition view. Photo: Nicholas Thomas.

they were suffering acutely, and surrendered works or valuables which they would not otherwise have chosen to dispose of. However, illegitimate acquisitions of these kinds are behind a comparatively small proportion of collections, though sometimes a high proportion of material from specific places. The stereotypic view recognizes neither the two- or multi-sided nature of relationships and entanglements salient to the formation of collections, nor the heterogeneity of Indigenous practice, such as the fact that ritual assemblages in Melanesia, for example, were frequently made for one-off ceremonial use and then disposed of. When people took the opportunity to sell them to collectors rather than simply throwing them away, or made such assemblages in response to demand, collecting was a scene of innovation and exchange, not one of appropriation.

15. Nor is it recognized that anthropological findings and collections are not dismissed by Indigenous people as appropriations, but – in many different ways – treated as resources, even as heritage. Anthropological reports from the colonial period are regarded as compendia of customary knowledge; historic artefacts are vital and empowering reference points for makers and artists, as well as eloquent expressions of ancestral creativity.

16. Similarly, the vision of the ethnographic museum as warehouse of colonial loot is oblivious of the collaborative practice which has not only been business as usual for some decades but, at the most progressive institutions, the very heart of the institution. While source community visits were once vital and catalytic exceptions to the usual routines of museum work, they are now, in the busiest institutions, part of that routine and may be happening every month if not every week. Co-produced exhibitions may at best be media for their values and narratives. Dialogue similarly informs open and critical reflection on colonial history and specifically on the formation of collections. All ethnography museums are history museums, and many exhibitions have acknowledged and explored the senses in which they are museums of difficult histories.

17. Museums should (and do) encourage open and wide-ranging debate, and not be merely defensive in their responses to campaigns and claims for the return of artefacts, to which they have become increasingly receptive. But public political culture at present is typically unsupportive of meaningful dialogue. The museums of ethnography and world culture which were relatively marginalized for so long, because cultural hierarchies privileged collections of canonical western art, risk marginalization again because they are considered political embarrassments, as collections and institutions which should simply not exist.

18. Owing to ongoing austerity and to political challenges, the present is a moment of vulnerability for museums of world culture. Yet at the same time, museums of no other kind have either a greater capacity to respond, or are more responsive, to the global challenges that define our time. Our collections speak, more potently and eloquently, to the histories of globalization and the many conflicts those histories engender. The collections are moreover an archive of global, and especially Indigenous, environmental knowledge. What they have to tell us about care for inhabited sites, for local land, for rivers, for lagoons and the sea is yet to be widely researched and interpreted, but represents a remarkable resource for the rediscovery and reinvention of sustainable practice.

19. In this context, museums of ethnography and world culture emphatically need advocacy. Their public image is confused and too often negative. If they are to contribute, creatively and vitally, to the post-migrant societies we all inhabit, they need to position themselves ambitiously rather than defensively, and to communicate the open, inclusive, dialogical work that they engage in.

20. The museum should be conceived, not only as a building, a precinct, an exhibition venue, or an institution, but also as a network of activity. Much of what we do that is most inspiring is off-site or behind the scenes. It involves new travels and exchanges, outreach and partnerships. It is also the work we do that is out of public view, with Indigenous visitors, community representatives, artists and experts. Some of this surfaces in our public programmes, but most visitors are unaware that ethnographic collections have become realms of unpredictable, sometimes contentious but always fertile encounter.

When the Centre Pompidou opened in Paris in the late 1970s, its audacious architecture, which externalized and rendered visible the museum infrastructure, made the new institution instantly famous. In the ethnographic museum, cross-cultural relationships historically constituted our infrastructure. Those relationships were complex, empowered and constrained by colonial asymmetries. The post-ethnographic museum tries knowingly to re-energize such relationships, negotiating colonial legacies but also the many possibilities the collections offer diverse publics, locally and internationally. It this relationality that we need to turn inside out, to exhibit, to put at the heart of our public narrative.

*Acknowledgement. Many museum curators, academics and commentators have discussed questions referred to in this short comment. I have not included citations here, but a relevant literature is reviewed and acknowledged more extensively in my book* The Return of Curiosity *(London, 2016). I thank all those involved in the SWICH network and programmes for discussions which have informed the essay, especially Wayne Modest for insightful and stimulating comments on a draft, and Annie Coombes, as always.*

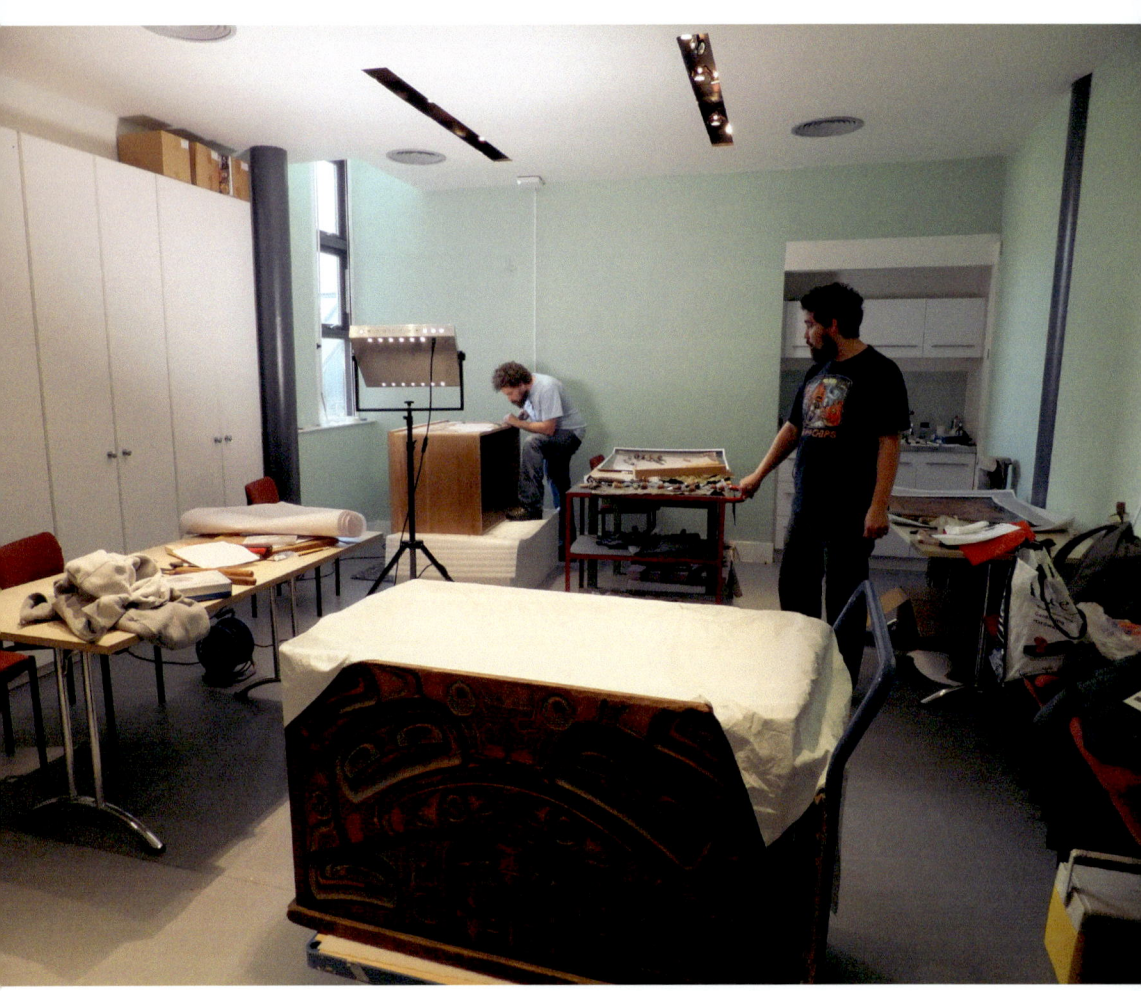

Fig. 2.1. Haida artists Gwaai Edenshaw and Jaalen Edenshaw replicating the 'Great Box' (Pitt Rivers Museum 1884.57.25), Pitt Rivers Museum, Oxford, 2014. Photograph by Laura Peers. Copyright Pitt Rivers Museum.

# *Museums and Source Communities*: Reflections and Implications

LAURA PEERS

*Museums and Source Communities* (Peers and Brown, 2003) has been widely cited since its publication in 2003. Part of a powerful shift among museums internationally to better understand the communities they serve and the nature of their relationships with those groups, the volume highlights forms of collaboration and consultation, documents the kinds of relationships emerging between museums and various communities of origin for collections, and considers the implications of such relationships for processes of curation. It has become a key reference in museum anthropology, with the introduction reprinted in Sheila Watson's *Museums and Their Communities* (2007), and it is widely cited in literature on museology and museum anthropology. The volume helped to popularise the term 'source community', with more than two thousand references produced by a quick Google Scholar search for 'source community + museum'. Other key publications on the theme of museums and communities since 2003 have refined relevant concepts: Vivian Golding and Wayne Modest's (2013) *Museums and Communities: Curators, Collections and Collaboration* usefully examines the assumption of duality in the museum/community relationship and explores processes of collaboration, as does Elizabeth Crooke's (2007) *Museums and Community: Ideas, Issues and Challenges*. Numerous case studies from around the globe have also illustrated the crucial kinds of 'social work' (Golding and Modest 2013, 1) arising from Indigenous community engagement with heritage collections.

Fifteen years after publication, at a time when the politics of museum relations with communities are shifting rapidly – with Emmanuel Macron's promise to return heritage items to Africa (Sarr and Savoy 2018), the United Nations Declaration on the Rights of Indigenous Peoples now a standard part of the museum landscape, and Canada's Truth and Reconciliation Calls to Action (2015) moving forward into museum praxis – it is useful to reflect on the book's goals and contexts. In this chapter, I reflect on how *Museums and Source Communities* came into being, on how its core concept has developed, and its impacts. While these reflections are my own, I wish to acknowledge with admiration and gratitude Alison K. Brown's significant intellectual work as co-editor in shaping the book and co-author of its introductory essay.

My impetus for creating *Museums and Source Communities* was a sense of frustration arising from the disconnect between the extraordinary historic collections from North American Indigenous communities in British museums and those communities themselves. Having trained in Canada and worked with Indigenous communities, I arrived at the Pitt Rivers Museum (PRM) in Oxford in 1998 to find that few museum professionals in the United Kingdom and the larger European Union had any deep understanding of the urgency with which Indigenous communities wanted – and needed – access to heritage collections to strengthen identity and cultural practice. Some UK colleagues were working closely with Indigenous communities in nuanced and careful ways, but often to create knowledge or exhibitions for UK museums rather than to meet Indigenous needs. This seemed to be true for the entire range of museums in Britain, from local authority-run town and regional museums to the national and university museums. Given imperial and colonial histories, the earliest historic material culture from North American peoples is held in UK and EU museums – sometimes quite small institutions – and has been relatively inaccessible to the descendants of its makers. Much material was acquired in the late nineteenth century, during an era of intense pressure to assimilate Indigenous peoples: objects were collected and removed from Indigenous communities in a process parallel to the removal of Indigenous children from residential schools. In the latter half of the twentieth century, Indigenous cultural resurgence in North America has been fuelled by a desire to heal from the wounds caused by this era and by a determination to reclaim cultural practices and knowledge after the transmission of these was interrupted. Heritage items have been important repositories of knowledge, and learning from them has constituted a crucial part of stabilising identity and self-esteem – key elements of well-being critical for improved health – for Indigenous researchers and their communities (Peers 2013; Lincoln 2010; Adelson 2000, 110). Many Indigenous people feel a need to reconnect with and learn from ancestral items that had gone to museums, but have had difficulty finding those items (see Brown 2014, 156-92). The links between historic collections and the contemporary health of Indigenous communities were not widely discussed within museological practice in the United Kingdom or European Union, nor was there a strong sense of accountability to those communities. Indeed, I was advised by colleagues at several institutions that I should not invite Indigenous people from Canada to view collections at PRM, because 'they'd just cause trouble'.

At the same time, British social and political issues around immigrant populations, the disabled, and marginalised groups such as Roma did not exactly parallel the Canadian experience with Indigenous peoples, but they did share some dynamics with how museums in settler countries have engaged with Indigenous communities. In the 1990s, Canadian museology underwent profound shifts in relation to the politics of Indigeneity and postcolonialism, triggered by the furore over the exhibition *The Spirit Sings* and the resulting national Task Force on Museums and First Peoples (Phillips 2012; Hill and Nicks 1992). Museum staff undertook curatorial and exhibition work with the increasing understanding that Indigenous people had rights related to collections of heritage items, that repatriation was part of the standard work of museums, and that media and political pressure could be deployed against museums that failed to consult (and, increasingly, collaborate with) Indigenous communities. The dynamics during the 1990s and early 2000s were very different in the United Kingdom, where expectations that museums should consult with various audiences were driven by UK government policy (both national and locally devolved) and associated funding mechanisms; the profession did not embrace the idea of deep collaboration, the expectation that communities held rights in relation to collections, or the concept that museums existed to serve Indigenous and other source communities. During this period the UK heritage field broadly embraced concepts of social inclusivity, as museums were pushed by government, funding, and policy bodies to broaden their audiences and reach out to marginalised groups within Britain (Lynch and Alberti 2010, 19; Watson 2007, 15-16). Some museums created community advisory forums, panels, or other mechanisms to consult or collaborate with local communities on exhibitions, programming, and policy. Initially there was, however, little sense that such audiences were core ones for museums, that museums existed to serve them and their goals, or that communities that were inconveniently located on other continents needed to be approached in the same ways.

As a lecturer teaching museum anthropology (focusing on relations between museums and Indigenous peoples), it was clear that the nature of museum relationships with communities was emerging as central to museological theory after the publication of Ivan Karp, Christine Kreamer, and Steven Lavine's (1992) *Museums and Communities* and James Clifford's (1997) adaptation of the contact zone concept for museums. Both began to articulate the responsibilities of museums to make heritage accessible to communities, to work with communities, to listen to them. There were many articles about emerging praxis in this area, but no book had yet gathered them together for teaching or for advancing developments across the museum profession.

I wondered if such a publication could introduce a strong, clear phrase to encompass the core relationship between museums and the communities their collections came from, in order to increase the use of that idea within the museum profession and in related scholarship. Several such terms were emerging in the 1990s, including 'community of origin' and 'source community'. I felt the need for a very direct term that would move beyond the neutral fiction of 'stakeholders' (then popular in the cultural sector), which implies that all parties – museum, community of origin, diverse public audiences – have equal stakes in the outcomes of a relationship. But the stakes are not the same: for Indigenous peoples, access to heritage items can be healing in the aftermath of colonial histories; it is a form of sovereignty (Field 2008, 1), the regaining of which is linked to physical and cultural survival. A member of an Indigenous community negotiating a relationship with a museum holding ancestral treasures has far more at stake than museum staff or a (still) typically white, middle-class museum visitor in England. I hoped also to communicate that the concept of source communities applied to all museums, local authority and university, national and regional, natural history museums and social history museums, 'ethnographic' museums and town museums. All hold heritage items from many communities, including overseas communities, and as such need to accept responsibility for providing access to heritage items to those communities as part of their core mandates.

As Brown and I (2003, 2) noted in the introduction to the volume:

> The term 'source communities' (sometimes referred to as 'originating communities') refers both to these groups in the past when artefacts were collected, as well as to their descendants today. These terms have most often been used to refer to indigenous peoples in the Americas and the Pacific, but apply to every cultural group from whom museums have collected: local people, diaspora and immigrant communities, religious groups, settlers, and indigenous peoples, whether those are First Nations, Aboriginal, Maori, or Scottish. Most importantly, the concept recognises that artefacts play an important role in the identities of source community members, that source communities have legitimate moral and cultural stakes or forms of ownership in museum collections, and that they may have special claims, needs, or rights of access to material heritage held by museums. In this new relationship, museums become stewards of artefacts on behalf of source communities. They are no longer the sole voices of authority in displaying and interpreting those objects, but acknowledge a moral and ethical (and sometimes political) obligation to involve source communities in decisions affecting their material heritage.

## Reflections on the Term 'Source Community' and Its Development Since 2003

Looking back, this characterisation captured key historical processes involved with such collections, especially for Indigenous and marginalised peoples. It also seems essentialist, as it fails to acknowledge the agency of many community members, emphasising instead only unequal relations of power involved in extractive collecting. The term therefore fails to capture the intentions or the complicated modernity and identity of Makareti Papakura, a Maori woman also known as Mrs Staples-Brown, who donated Maori items from her marital home in Oxfordshire to the Pitt Rivers Museum to be ambassadors for Maori culture.

The emphasis on extractive collecting also subsumes the many complex paths through which objects arrived at museums. The term does not entirely accommodate the origins of the Newton Turvey collection at the Pitt Rivers Museum, part of which was made by Lakota women travelling with a Wild West show who met and taught beadwork to an admiring Englishman, Newton Turvey, and sold him finished and half-finished items, which Turvey finished. Some of the material is made entirely by Lakota hands, and descendants of the makers have asked for photographs in order to replicate it for family use. Other items in the collection are made partly by Lakota women and partly by Turvey, and still others were made entirely by Turvey. For Lakotas, all of the material is intellectually Lakota, since it all involves family designs and techniques, and Lakotas consider themselves to be the source community for the collection, but the cross-cultural relationships involved are not encompassed by the concept. The term 'source community' works strongly for Haida ancestral items, collected from Haida people on Haida Gwaii, although collectors seldom specified the village, moiety, clan, names, status, or occupational identity of people from whom items were acquired, making 'the Haida' sound more monolithic than they were. 'Source community' is less clear for other objects. Some historic Indigenous groups included wives from very different cultural groups, and while one can identify an object from, say, the plains Cree, the beadwork may have been done by an Ojibwa wife. What community is it from? The 'witch in the bottle' in the PRM collections was associated by its English collectors with a working class, regional and rural community of origin, but it is also an English object. The middle-class academics who were keen to acquire such 'folk' survivals would not have seen themselves as members of the same English 'source community'.

The concept of 'source communities' thus essentialises identities and communities, implying that there is a homogenous thing called a community, bounded and uniform in terms of identity, from which an object arises, and that such objects are expected to be purely English, or Haida, or Lakota. Such concepts of boundedness and homogeneity have spurred widespread critiques of the concept of 'community' across the social sciences for some decades (see, for example, Brint 2001; Amit and Rapport 2002; Young 1986). While some scholars have moved away from the term for these reasons, it persists as a fundamental organising principle in the social sciences and in popular usage. The *Annual Review of Anthropology* has offered articles about many kinds of communities, ranging from online communities to relationships between archaeological sites and descendant communities (e.g., Wilson and Peterson 2002; Bell 2017, Colwell 2016); and at Benedict Anderson's (2006) urging, scholars have considered nations as 'imagined communities'. As Gerd Baumann (1996, 4) realised during fieldwork among a complex multicultural community in London, 'community was a concept to be used and redefined contextually, but certainly it could not be written off as an irrelevancy'. Source communities are complex, but they are real, and we need to be wary of theory-based dismissals of the concept that fail to take on board lived, experiential realities. Indigenous peoples today are encountering anomie in museums due to perceptions – rooted in scholarly critique – that source communities are too diverse and complex to consult meaningfully (Sherry Farrell-Racette, personal communication, 2018). 'Community' is what binds humans together across their diversities, and the concept is valid to people who consider themselves to be part of various communities.

Work since 2003 has refined thinking about the nature of 'community' linked to museums, including Watson's (2007, 4) discussion of communities as defined by shared historical or cultural experiences, specialist knowledge, or demographic/socioeconomic factors. All of these issues might come into play for different Indigenous members of a community. With regards to heritage items, the term 'source community' must encompass, rather than exclude, the nuances inherent in community and identity. Taking Canadian Indigenous groups as an example, the concept of a source community such as Haida or Anishinaabeg includes persons with diverse perspectives and aspects of identity across different generations. It includes people who do speak and those who do not speak an Indigenous language, those who were removed during the Sixties Scoop and those who were raised in cities or on reserves. It includes residential school survivors and youth educated in community-run language immersion schools, people who feel they 'don't know much about their culture' as the result of generations of assimilation and those who have fought to retain cultural practices, and Christians and spiritual practitioners who are more traditionally oriented.

For all the refinements and critiques it has undergone, the term still usefully insists that there are groups of people who maintain relationships with heritage items in museums, and that items in overseas museum collections are tangible heritage, with all the politics and potential that implies. This is the element in which I remain most interested intellectually: the social and spiritual links between historic museum collections and contemporary social networks and cultural practices and identities, the meanings and potencies of historic material culture in the present, and the implications of these issues for museums.

For Indigenous people, relationships with ancestral items are profoundly social, for many different reasons. For some, objects are understood as actively or potentially animate beings embodied in material form and requiring social interaction; for others, they are material manifestations of cultural knowledge and history, calling to mind ancestors whose difficult lives enabled their descendants to exist in the present; for still others, objects engage the social networks in which knowledge of their materials, making, and associated cultural contexts is embedded. Such understandings challenge museological definitions of 'objects' and assumptions about who the museum is for. They provoke deeply affective responses: weeping on and with objects; playful performative handling by miming the intended uses of items; and storytelling, song, and dance. Through all of these, community members articulate both the joy of reconnection and the grief and anger of historical loss (Collison 2013, 187-89; Phillips 2005, 96-97; Brown and Peers 2015, 264; Lynch 2011, 150). These engagements also involve museum staff as mediators and gatekeepers. Staff are often included in performance and ritual involving ancestral items, and such moments can be profoundly moving and transformative for them.[1] These

---

1   Encounters between Indigenous researchers and university students are also transformative for students, grounding theoretical readings and inspiring powerful learning moments. As a curator with teaching responsibilities, I have always invited visiting Indigenous researchers at PRM to speak to staff and students and have invited students to assist in many capacities during research visits. It has meant a great deal to Indigenous researchers to be able to teach at Oxford, to be able to speak in such a place, and it has similarly meant much to the students to learn directly from those engaged in such work and to witness the emotions and passion such work entails.

moments are consciously intended to teach staff why such access to collections matters (Peers 2017), and about the obligation of museums to relatives, both the living who visit and those we care for in the form of ancestral treasures in museum collections: we are being taught about the relationship of obligation inherent in the phrase 'source community'.

This relationship of obligation, or responsibility, has since 2003 also been addressed in the literature on heritage and cultural property. While there are concerns with conflating Western legal systems of property with the Indigenous moral and ethical expectations involved in museum collections, discussions in the cultural property literature have moved into useful areas. As Jane Anderson and Haidy Geismar (2018) state in their introduction to the *Routledge Companion to Cultural Property*, the phrase cultural property is 'used to describe ways of talking about collective entitlement, shared inheritance, the material nature of identity'. They write that their task is to examine 'this category of inalienable relationship between the state and its possessions. . . . The language of cultural property has been adopted and adapted by collectivities that actively resist the authority of the state over diverse cultural resources' (2018, 1). A section in the volume entitled 'Museums, Archives and Communities' suggests the durability and continued utility of the concept of the relationships between these entities. Their introductory essay resonates with a statement made to Alison Brown and me by the late Kainai elder Andy Blackwater about his sense of connection to Blackfoot ancestral items in UK museums: 'You are holding part of us there. We don't alienate ourselves from those items. We continue to include them in our prayers' (Brown and Peers 2015, 268).

Literature since the publication of *Museums and Source Communities* has explored significant difficulties inherent in its core messages. Bernadette Lynch and Sam Alberti (2010) and Robin Boast (2011) discuss the continuing inequities of power in relationships between museums and source communities, the failure of museums to serve the goals of source communities, and the ways that museums appear to offer access and support to communities while continuing to control access, voice, knowledge, and representation. Developing a perspective voiced by Tony Bennett in 1998, such critiques see the contact zone less as 'a space for cross-cultural dialogues and source community expertise' and more as 'an extension of the museum as an instrument of governmentality, expressed as multiculturalism' (Boast 2011, 59). Their concerns are summed up in Boast's (2011, 67) caveat that 'the new museum, the museum as contact zone, is and continues to be used instrumentally as a means of masking. . . fundamental asymmetries, appropriations, and biases'. These critiques focus on how museums control the participation of communities within the 'invited space' of the museum (Lynch and Alberti 2010, 14). Far less literature examines such engagements from the perspectives of source community members, and what there is looks very different from mainstream museological and museum anthropological work. As an example, one might note that rather than theoretical critiques of 'community', 'contact zones' or 'invited spaces', 'source communities' or 'decolonisation', or the severe budgetary and difficult governance constraints faced by many local authority museums in the United Kingdom, the 2018 meeting of the US Association of Tribal Archives, Libraries, and Museums includes sessions on collections risk assessment, negotiating the Native American Graves Protection and Repatriation Act (NAGPRA), grant writing, digitisation projects on a budget, respectful handling and storage of sacred items, and safeguarding cultural heritage from theft (see http://www.atalm.org). In refining understandings of the relationships between museums and source communities, we need to focus more clearly on the different goals, needs, opportunities, and pressures faced by both parties. Boast's caveat about differential relations of power involved in the relationships between museums and source communities is true at fundamental levels.

I disagree, however, with Boast's statement (2011, 63) that 'no matter how much we try to make the spaces accommodating, they remain sites where the Others come to perform for us, not with us'. This disregards the agency of Indigenous researchers who come in ever-increasing numbers, usually self-funded, to museums across the United Kingdom and European Union to pursue their own goals. To use just one example, the Great Box Project (https://www.prm.ox.ac.uk/haidabox), in which Haida artists Gwaai and Jaalen Edenshaw came to the Pitt Rivers Museum to replicate an ancestral masterpiece, fulfilled the artists' dual goals of learning from the master artist of the box and repatriating a masterpiece for use within the community. The project also served the goals of the funding agencies and of the host museum (being featured, for instance, with the artists' permission, on the cover of PRM's annual report). Source community researchers such as these are not 'performing' for museums, and they are often experienced at working with museums and fully aware of museums' desire to use these visits as ethical capital. I also feel that Lynch and Alberti's position on museums as 'invited spaces' fails to fully consider the determination of Indigenous source communities who accept invitations and engage with museums, but with their own goals and on their own terms, with a sophisticated understanding of the political dynamics involved.

### *Museums and Source Communities*: Applied Praxis

For me, the phrase 'source communities' was a means to a key goal, encouraging museums to see themselves as responsible to those communities, just as they are responsible for the care of collections. In acting on the philosophy and overarching goals of the book, I have endeavoured to bridge in my own curatorial practice the enormous geographical, political and cultural gaps between Indigenous communities in North America and the Pitt Rivers Museum in Oxford, and to work in alignment with the goals of Indigenous peoples. Working with Alison Brown,

Fig. 2.2. The 'Great Box' (PRM 1884.57.25) and its child, Pitt Rivers Museum, Oxford, 2014. Photograph by Robert Rapoport. Copyright Pitt Rivers Museum.

Cara Krmpotich, and others, I have explored collaborative forms of research that meets museum, scholarly, and community needs. Specific projects have included returning copies of historic photographs from PRM to the Kainai (Blackfoot) people to understand what such images mean to them in the present (Brown, Peers, and Members of the Kainai Nation, 2006) and developing enhanced loans, by inviting community members to handle and learn from historic objects before the loan items are exhibited at the host venue. In one project, five Blackfoot shirts collected in 1841 were lent to museums in Blackfoot territory and over five hundred Blackfoot people were able to reconnect with them, before exhibitions at the host venues and back at PRM (Peers and Brown 2016). Other work has involved supporting visiting Indigenous artists researching historic techniques with PRM collections, and a large delegation of Haida Nation members who worked with hundreds of ancestral treasures at PRM and the British Museum (Krmpotich and Peers 2013). These focused projects also ranged outwards, including conferences bringing groups of UK museum professionals together with members of a community whose heritage they steward; claims for and eventual repatriation of ancestral remains; and the making of the Great Box's 'child' to be taken home for use in the community. These have been powerful engagements, opening dialogue and creating opportunities for museum colleagues to learn directly from Indigenous community representatives about the complexity and broadness of colonial collections, about their meanings past and present, and about Indigenous perspectives on material heritage and its links to postcolonial healing. They, and parallel initiatives by colleagues across the United Kingdom and European Union and internationally, have demonstrated an acceptance of the responsibility of museums toward source communities to support such healing through forms of access to collections, including study visits, digitisation, remaking, and repatriation.

The complex logistics of such projects ground and articulate the more abstract concepts embedded in the concept of 'source community'. Tellingly, all of the logistics needed to do this work seem to challenge the expectations and professional standards embedded in museums. Staff need to create new handling protocols to facilitate sensory reconnection with ancestral items, and new processes for financial reimbursement (with per diem payments up front, preferably in cash, to support visiting community members who may not have the finances to get them through a visit and claim afterwards). Smoke detectors need to be disabled in order to enable Indigenous research visitors to smudge for protection and purification. Staff hosting delegates who may not have travelled overseas before need to find ways of supporting the group, including attending meals with the group out of standard work hours or working on weekends (and persuade finance officers that their meals need to be reimbursed for this work). Short-notice visits sometimes happen when Indigenous researchers budget and plan for an overseas trip to Museum A, but find that Museum B in the same country has an important collection: if museums are indeed serving communities, they need to support such requests for access to collections as best they can rather than refusing them on the grounds of insufficient advance notice.

These are real issues, but they are also surface difficulties masking deeper structural impediments to change. We might wonder why special projects always rely on external funding, and why funding applications need to be written in the language of scholarly research or foundation agendas in order to fund activities designed to meet community needs. Why can museum budgets routinely pay for IT or educational staff, but not for bringing source community members to the museum to work with staff and collections? Why do some museums have difficulty accepting that a history of encounters between local people and overseas groups means a responsibility today to provide Indigenous groups access? (On Britain's colonial aphasia affecting such perceptions, see Edwards [2018].) We might wonder why scholars have to make the argument (as we did to the Leverhulme Trust for the Haida project) that culture-bearers are equal to academic scholars (which the Trust accepted, but the argument had to be made). We might consider the hierarchical and departmental structures of power and territory within museums, which sometimes prevent staff from cooperating effectively to support all aspects of Indigenous research visits. Given the complex preparations for and facilitation of such visits, members of different museum staff teams may find themselves working together in the same room for the first time during such visits. We might consider the question of routine invigilation of research visits and the issues of ownership, authority, and the issues of power and control these raise when Indigenous source community members engage with heritage items in the museum space. We might also consider the museological control over knowledge and authority in the construction of museum records and the extent to which expert source community members are permitted to influence these (and see, on such issues, Brown 2016).

To begin to change the structural dynamics museums have inherited, staff might question and critically appraise the information that came with historic collections when museums acquired them, and consider with members of communities of origin how they might wish to respond to the ethnocentrism, racism, inaccuracies, and misunderstandings that such texts and comments typically articulate. We might ask members of source communities who are learning about their cultural heritage through museums as a result of colonialism what they wish to learn and how museum staff can support them. We might ask if we can supply images of objects in museums for language-learning classes to support endangered Indigenous languages, and we should certainly ask what community members want to say to the world about their heritage through museum displays and educational programmes. And we should take their comments seriously, even when we are uncomfortable with them. Working with source communities needs to be seen as an integral and essential part of collections care and a way to develop conversations between disparate museum audiences by enlivening exhibitions and programming. This should be true of all museums, not just 'ethnographic' ones or those with substantial 'world cultures' collections.

As Boast (2011) and Lynch and Alberti (2010) have noted, the key issue in relationships between museums and source communities is power. Museums may have begun to engage with source communities at the curatorial or programming level, but have not really done so in the United Kingdom and European Union at the governance level. The demographics of museum staff, directors, and board members do not reflect the origins of museum collections or the museum's responsibilities to source communities. No one on staff is formally tasked with maintaining relationships developed after an externally funded project with a source community ends, or the curator responsible for the project is expected to do that informally (Brown 2016; Brown and Peers 2015, 282). Quite often, images from such projects are deployed as ethical capital by museums in conference presentations, annual reports, and funding documents and on websites – quite legitimately - but without routinely sending these images to community members so that they can do the same, or with the same attention to source community needs and goals. These patterns indicate that museums have not yet accepted Watson's observation (2007, 9) that '[t]he relationship museums have with their communities must be based on the recognition that this is an unequal one, with the balance of power heavily tipped in favour of the institution'.

These difficulties, like the difficulties of working with source communities in all their complexity and diversity, do not mean that we cannot do this work; they indicate that such work is necessary. We need to embed this work in museum practice and in the training of museum staff. We need to make sure that every museum has a core, long-term staff member whose job description is 'community liaison', charged with maintaining relationships and a sense of community goals and finding ways the museum might meet them. We need to document the effects of community engagements on museums and on community partners, to find measures of efficacy of such work, and to respond to and influence funding bodies and institutional and government policies.

My own measures of efficacy for the work of museums and source communities are not easily quantified: 'impact' for such work is not about numbers. Measures of success in this work include watching a younger museum colleague, who was terrified at the thought of Haida performative handling of collections, learning to support and facilitate such handling. They also include watching a young, emerging Haida leader nervously give his first keynote speech to a group of museum professionals gathered at Oxford, and then watching over time as he has taken on an important leadership role in his community. They include laughter as historic gambling sticks were used to gamble within a museum research space, and the sound of drums resonating through the museum's building. They include a Blackfeet college student who, after encountering powerful ancestral shirts, changed his college major to focus on Blackfeet art and went on to a national art college. They include moments of incredible tension as a fragile historic Blackfoot shirt was folded and passed reverently between men to revive a ceremony once illegal under assimilation policies. They include seeing the Great Box's child used as it was meant to be, as a box of clan treasures in a potlatch, and a toddler dancing in front of it as she was given her Haida name: witnessing an ancestral treasure removed from museum control and doing exactly what assimilation policies tried to destroy.

Moira Simpson (2009, 128) writes of 'museums as supporting actors in communities'. I would add that they have an obligation to be such supporting actors, and that source communities are also supporting actors in museums. That museological and Indigenous dialogues and relationships are now turning – after UNDRIP and Macron, after the calls for action following Canada's Truth and Reconciliation Commission – to repatriation and to the need for museum collections to serve as 'an active site of claim making that is about political recognition, cultural memory, and identity formation' (Anderson and Geismar 2018), demonstrates the continuing potency of relations between museums and source communities.

## References

Adelson, Naomi. 2000. *'Being Alive Well': Health and the Politics of Cree Well-being*. Toronto: University of Toronto Press.

Amit, Vered, and Nigel Rapport. 2002. *The Trouble with Community: Anthropological Reflections on Movement, Identity and Collectivity*. London: Pluto.

Anderson, Benedict. 2006. *Imagined Communities: Reflections on the Origin and Spread of Nationalism*. London: Verso Books.

Anderson, Jane, and Haidy Geismar. 2018. 'Introduction'. In *Routledge Companion to Cultural Property*. London: Routledge. Accessed 10 August 2018. https://www.routledge.com/The-Routledge-Companion-to-Cultural-Property/Anderson-Geismar/p/book/9781138812642.

Baumann, Gerd. 1996. *Contesting Culture: Discourses of Identity in Multi-ethnic London*. Cambridge: Cambridge University Press.

Bell, Joshua A. 2017. 'A Bundle of Relations: Collections, Collecting, and Communities'. *Annual Review of Anthropology* 46: 241-49.

Boast, Robin. 2011. 'Neocolonial Collaboration: Museum as Contact Zone Revisited'. *Museum Anthropology* 34, no. 1: 56-70.

Brint, Steven. 2001. 'Gemeinschaft Revisited: A Critique and Reconstruction of the Community Concept'. *Sociological Theory* 19, no. 1: 1-23.

Brown, Alison K. 2014. *First Nations, Museums, Narrations: Stories of the 1929 Franklin Motor Expedition to the Canadian Prairies*. Vancouver: UBC Press.

Brown, Alison K. 2016. 'Co-Authoring Relationships: Blackfoot Collections, UK Museums, and Collaborative Practice'. *Collaborative Anthropologies* 9, no. 1: 117-48.

Brown, Alison K., and Laura Peers. 2006. *Pictures Bring Us Messages / Sinaakssiiksi Aohtsimaahpihkookiyaawa: Photographs and Histories from the Kainai Nation*. Toronto: University of Toronto Press.

Brown, Alison K., and Laura Peers. 2015. 'The Blackfoot Shirts Project: "Our Ancestors Have Come to Visit"'. In *Museums in Transformation: Dynamics of Democratization and Decolonization*, edited by Annie E. Coombes and Ruth B. Phillips, 263-87. The International Handbooks of Museum Studies. Oxford: Wiley Blackwell.

Clifford, James. 1997. 'Museums as Contact Zones'. In *Routes: Travel and Translation in the Late Twentieth Century*, 188-219. Cambridge, MA: Harvard University Press.

Collison, Nika. 2013. 'Giving Life to Our Treasures: Handling Does Not Lead to Damage'. In *This Is Our Life: Haida Material Heritage and Changing Museum Practice*, edited by Cara Krmpotich and Laura Peers, 187-89. Vancouver: UBC Press.

Colwell, Chip. 2016. 'Collaborative Archaeologies and Descendant Communities'. *Annual Review of Anthropology* 45, no. 1: 113-27.

Crooke, Elizabeth. 2007. *Museums and Community: Ideas, Issues and Challenges*. London: Routledge.

Edwards, Elizabeth. 2018. 'Addressing Colonial Narratives in Museums'. *The British Academy* (blog). 19 April. https://www.thebritishacademy.ac.uk/blog/addressing-colonial-narratives-museums, accessed 6 May 2019.

Field, Les W. 2008. *Abalone Tales: Collaborative Explorations of Sovereignty and Identity in Native California*. Durham, NC: Duke.

Golding, Vivian, and Wayne Modest, eds. 2013. *Museums and Communities: Curators, Collections and Collaboration*. London: Bloomsbury.

Hill, Tom, and Trudy Nicks, eds. 1992. *Turning the Page: Task Force Report on Museums and First Peoples*. Accessed 28 August 2018. https://museums.in-1touch.org/uploaded/web/docs/Task_Force_Report_1994.pdf.

Karp, Ivan, Christine Kreamer, and Steven D. Lavine, eds. 1992. *Museums and Communities: The Politics of Public Culture*. Washington, DC: Smithsonian Institution Press.

Krmpotich, Cara, and Laura Peers. 2013. *This Is Our Life: Haida Material Heritage and Changing Museum Practice*. Vancouver: UBC Press.

Lincoln, Amber. 2010. 'Body Techniques of Health: Making Products and Shaping Selves in Northwest Alaska'. *Etudes Inuits/STUDIES* 34, no. 2: 39-50.

Lynch, Bernadette T. 2011. 'Collaboration, Contestation, and Creative Conflict: On the Efficacy of Museum/Community Partnerships'. In *The Routledge Companion to Museum Ethics: Redefining Ethics for the Twenty-first Century Museum*, edited by Janet Marstine, 146-63. London: Routledge.

Lynch, Bernadette T., and Samuel J. Alberti. 2010. 'Legacies of Prejudice: Racism, Co-production and Radical Trust in the Museum'. *Museum Management and Curatorship* 25, no. 1: 13-35.

Peers, Laura. 2013. '"Ceremonies of Renewal": Visits, Relationships, and Healing in the Museum Space'. *Museum Worlds* 1, no. 1: 136-52.

Peers, Laura. 2017. 'The Magic of Bureaucracy'. *Museum Worlds* 5, no. 1: 9-21.

Peers, Laura, and Alison K. Brown. 2003. *Museums and Source Communities: A Routledge Reader*. London: Routledge.

Peers, Laura, and Alison K. Brown. 2016. *Visiting with the Ancestors: Blackfoot Shirts in Museum Spaces*. Edmonton: Athabasca University Press.

Phillips, Ruth B. 2005. 'Re-placing Objects: Historical Practices for the Second Museum Age'. *Canadian Historical Review* 86: 83-110.

Phillips, Ruth B. 2012. 'Moment of Truth: The Spirit Sings as Critical Event and the Exhibition Inside It'. In *Museum Pieces: Towards the Indigenization of Canadian Museums*, 48-70. Montreal: McGill-Queen's University Press.

Sarr, Felwine, and Bénédicte Savoy. 2018. *Rapport sur la restitution du patrimoine culturel africain. Vers une nouvelle éthique relationnelle.* Ministry of Culture, France. http://restitutionreport2018.com.

Simpson, Moira. 2009. 'Museums and Restorative Justice: Heritage, Repatriation and Cultural Education'. *Museum International* 61, no. 1-2: 121-29.

Truth and Reconciliation Commission of Canada (TRC). 2015. *Calls to Action 2015*. www.trc.ca/websites/trcinstitution/File/2015/Findings/Calls_to_Action_English2.pdf.

Watson, Sheila. 2007. 'Introduction'. In *Museums and Their Communities*, edited by Sheila Watson, 1-23. London: Routledge.

Wilson, Samuel M., and Leighton C. Peterson. 2002. 'The Anthropology of Online Communities'. *Annual Review of Anthropology* 31: 449-467.

Young, Iris M. 1986. 'The Ideal of Community and the Politics of Difference'. *Social Theory and Practice* 12, no. 1: 1-26.

# Collaboration and the Dilemma of the Exotic: A Research Note

BARBARA PLANKENSTEINER

In this chapter I would like to explore questions related to collaborative practices between museums of ethnography or world cultures, and the so-called source and migrant communities in those museums' immediate surroundings. Such practices have aimed to facilitate encounters not only with objects but between people, and to give voice to other perspectives on museum collections and narratives. Equally, collaborative contemporary art projects, which have taken place at or in these museums or in art institutions, have adopted comparable approaches in which artists envision immersive environments by getting deeply involved in other cultural spheres of knowledge and living, and, as a result, to co-create collaborative artscapes together with members of these communities. Such approaches usually are intended to allow audiences to experience difference and appreciate other values, including through encounters with the 'real' people involved.

In what follows I want to examine examples of such practices. My aim is to stimulate critical reflection about what I would call here 'the right of self-exoticization' as a mode of self-representation, the production of difference, the celebration of diversity, and the role and impact of ethnographic museums as a stage for such cultural encounters. This essay is therefore preliminary; it is an assemblage of thoughts and questions for future speculation, rather than a thorough analytical treatise of the matter.[1] That said, I will suggest avenues of connection with existing bodies of research that have addressed similar themes.

In 2014, Christian Kravagna, an art historian and professor of postcolonial studies in Vienna, criticised the Weltmuseum Wien in response to some of the exhibition projects of the museum, denouncing them as colonialist and accusing the museum of performing folklore. Kravagna referred to events promoted and programmed by the museum that resulted from collaborations with local migrant communities or embassies. These cultural festivities had been planned, organised, and financed by the embassies or community associations. Examples of these included the Nigerian Adire festival, a Día de los Muertos celebration organised by members of the Vienna Mexican community, and an exhibition that also featured live rituals performed by Bon priests. The museum offered the space for these events and did not influence the groups' proposed programmes. The criticism from Kravagna did not refer to any specific event, but rather was a generic questioning of this kind of programme, that was, by his account, metonymic for a colonialist practice.

At the time, I wrote a response defending this practice of collaboration by pointing out that ethnographic museums should give room for self-representation (Plankensteiner 2015). I described these sorts of cultural festivals as the self-deter-

---

1  An earlier version of this text was presented as paper at a SWICH [Sharing a World of Inclusion, Creativity and Heritage] conference at the Museum Volkenkunde in Leiden in 2016. I thank Wayne Modest for the many suggestions to rework these thoughts that still are in a preliminary state and need further elaboration and theoretical grounding.

mined and self-confident initiatives of communities who were taking the opportunity to 'claim' space in a cultural institution in the centre of a metropolis, which was in stark contrast to the usual spaces at the margins of the city where these groups would usually celebrate important occasions. But even while defending these practices, I was disquieted; I had experienced some reservations and uneasiness when I participated in some of these events that in many respects questioned and inverted our values as curators and museums, and intellectual discourses about representation, Othering, exoticising, and the production of difference in the history of our institutions.

While I still believe that ethnographic museums should offer a space for such encounters and for self-determined cultural representation, I have begun to wonder if such collaborative formats need a sort of curation. What kind of mentoring or monitoring could the museum offer? Would such an effort again be a mechanism of control, paternalism, and asymmetric power relations within the museum sphere, which we were working to dismantle in recent years? How might the backdrop of such museums, with their colonial legacy and their audiences' eagerness to encounter the exotic, impact such endeavours toward self-representation? Should these events, even if they are not curated, nonetheless be 'allowed' because they coincide with a vision of cultural representation and collaboration that is embedded in the museum, even if they are internally and externally critiqued by some? I do not pretend here to have answers to these questions, but I would like to at least provoke some thinking around these issues.

I would like to clarify my concerns by presenting some of the instances that caused my own disquiet about this conundrum of exoticisation vs self-exoticisation within the museum space and comparing them with historical examples of exhibiting peoples within exhibitionary institutions[2]. The examples I present here encompass a diverse range of collaborations, all of which included interactions with the public. While such public-facing collaborations have become commonplace in world culture museums and are often understood as ways to reinterpret the museum as a 'contact zone', there has not been much analytical reflection on the ramifications of such programmes. In reviewing them more closely, they raise issues around the (self-) construction of identities, especially in relation to idealisations of the 'ecological noble savage', stereotypical and reductionist representations of cultures used in touristic imagery and national diplomatic representations, and the appropriation of religious practices along with the sacralisation of museum spaces. My overview is not meant to denounce these contemporary practices but rather elicit reflection on their significance and the challenges they pose in our contemporary museum work.

---

2   I use exhibitionary here in reference to Tony Bennett's (1995) exhibitionary complex, an entangled field of exhibitionary institutions including world fairs, colonial exhibitions, etc.

## Three Case Studies

In 2013, the Weltmuseum Wien organised an exhibition and live performance together with the art history department at Vienna University in the framework of a research project (Klimburg-Salter, Lojda, and Ramble 2013). It was titled *BÖN. Spirits in Butter. Art and Ritual of Old Tibet*. Lama Yangön Sherab Tenzin from the Samling monastery (Nepal), a tantric spiritual head and lineage master of the Bon religion, came for the first time to Vienna to conduct a series of 'traditional rituals', as they were called, and live performances at the museum. As part of the exhibition, a group of Bon priests from Nepalese and French monasteries created an altar, on which it was said the gods of their religion would dwell. The rituals could be experienced live in the museum or streamed online.

One of the marketing slogans urged potential visitors to 'experience religious rituals first-hand [*hautnah*] in the museum!' The project co-curator and professor for Asian art at Vienna University Deborah Klimburg-Salter underscored that this was not a show or a spectacle, but rather the performance of *real* rituals. The audience was invited to ask the priests questions, create prayer flags under their supervision, and actively participate in the rituals, including receiving blessings and being purified. For more than a month, an exhibition of rare examples of Bon art framed the specially created altar where the ceremonies took place and visitors could observe them.

Steven Engelsman, the museum director at the time, said in an interview that the exhibition meant a lot to the museum because it was a purification ceremony that would drive away evil spirits from the building to make it ready for a new beginning and for a soon-to-start renovation. A closing ritual in association with the Tibetan New Year celebrations was performed to liberate the community from negative forces, and it offered to free museum visitors from the baggage of the past year. This ritual was performed in several stages including a smoke ceremony, a fire sacrifice, Cham dances, and the destruction of an effigy.

Christian Schicklgruber, the museum curator in charge of the exhibition, and the whole staff of the museum took great care to respectfully follow the priests' instructions and to fulfil their needs. Although the priests were in charge and directed the procedure, their actions where commented upon and announced to the public and the press by the curators who acted as cultural brokers. We have no first-hand account from the priests regarding how they experienced their stay and interactions at the museum and whether the experience fulfilled their expectations.

How should we understand this kind of ritual performance in the museum? Is it the reinforcement or continuation of earlier exoticising practices, or should we acknowledge the agency of the Nepalese partners in their own self-performance? Does the ethnographic museum overdetermine any possibility for such practices to be viewed otherwise? What role did the ceremony play for the museum itself and the audience? Was it a spectacle that was successful in drawing a large crowd into the museum or a moving religious experience of renewal and relief?

Rituals accompanying opening or closing ceremonies have become a frequent practice within collaborative museum work. Prominent exhibition projects featuring Pacific arts, like the large Oceania exhibition at the Royal Academy that opened in September 2018 or the Pacific Encounters exhibition of 2006, also in the UK, were all 'endorsed' by an initial ceremonial 'activation' of the works of art on display. The curators of the exhibition saw this practice as enriching the experience for all involved – the visitors, museum staff, and descendants of the groups of people from whom the works originated – because it increased understanding of the inherent value of objects as embodied ancestors for descendant groups, as well as fostering a deeper appreciation of the art (Hooper et al. 2012). These practices are also part of honouring ancestors. While including these rituals might be of great value for building new relationships, such sacralisation of the museum space and the resacralisation of objects can also lead to friction if they are used as gestures of politicised religiosity, as Saloni Mathur and Kavita Singh (2017) point out with reference to Indian museums getting enmeshed in religious identity politics. Mathur and Singh (2017, 150) write that there is a definite need for cultural institutions to respond to such shifting ideas of the role of museums, as the boundary between the shrine and the museum are being blurred:

> the opposition between the realm of the sacred and the presumably secular, national space of the museum, a prevailing distinction in art history's understanding of museum formation in Europe, is a conceptual structure that no longer meets the theoretical challenges of museums today.

Collaborations with communities within the arena of world cultures museums can indeed be affected by the growing role of religion in politics and the drive toward self-representation by diverse groups.

Another event that took place at the Weltmuseum Wien in June 2013 was the Adire Festival organised by the National Association of the Nigerian Community in Austria (NANCA), in collaboration with the Embassy of the Nigerian Republic in Vienna. The museum had established a close relationship with the Nigerian community following two major exhibitions devoted to the art and cultural history of their country in the course of which I, as the curator, had reached out to members of the Nigerian community in Vienna to invite them to partake in programmes.

The Adire Festival had been proposed by the president of NANCA, Oluyemi Ogundele, who took great pains to make it happen and give his community prominence in a positive way. In the organisers' perception, the festival aimed to promote and celebrate African culture, heritage, and community cohesion amongst people from different backgrounds.

The festival, which took place over the course of a week, included a carnival procession through the city that ended with a party in the museum with prominent guests from Nigeria and cultural performances; a fashion show and a Nollywood festival; an Adire workshop with food stands offering Nigerian specialties; and the attendance of special guests such as David Alaba (FC Bayern München), Yemisi Rieger (Miss Vienna 2013), Rubin Okotie (FC Sturm Graz), several Nollywood stars, and people of political prominence from Nigeria.

The 'folkloric' performances included what might be regarded as a 'stereotypical' African image, with drummers and acrobats in 'exotic' animal-print outfits; there were similar stereotypical presentations of Chinese and Brazilian groups that had been invited to participate. However, the programme also presented contemporary Nigerian popular and celebrity culture, explored cultural traditions and demonstrated people's pride in them. The event was an invitation to Austrians to join in the celebrations, to respect and get to know Nigerian culture, and to accept Nigerian immigrants as rightful members of Austrian society. In this example, the museum offered the space for the occasion and had no active role in planning the event, except for offering a platform and publicising it through the museum's media channels.

The Nigerian community was very satisfied with the outcome of the festival but due to the fact that the Weltmuseum Wien was closed for renovation, a second edition of the event, which took place in 2016, could not be done at the museum but at a different location in Vienna. Looking at the crowd attending the event at the museum, it was clear that it attracted predominantly African-Austrians and did not reach the larger museum public. This could have been because the museum failed in publicising the event successfully, or it could also have been due to a lack of interest in such events among the museum's usual audience. Nevertheless, on the whole it was very well attended by members of the African diaspora.

In this example, the museum as a major and visible institution at the heart of a capital city acted as site for the celebration of culture and provided a space of empowerment for a marginalised group in society. Other similar self-organised festivals also exist in other cities. These follow a form of nation branding, drawing on specific imagined representation, even stereotypes, of the nation. Numerous scholars have analysed how national imaginaries are constructed through specific acts of performing the nation. Such nation-branding events are, however, also contested spaces; they are not sites that depict a finished notion of the nation, but rather are spaces of negotiating and contesting the representation of what the nation is or wants to become (see, for example, Guss 2000). Ethnographic museums have long battled with spectacular representations that portray cultures or nations as singular, fixed, or final. Can the temporality of such performances provide some insights into possible modes of museum representation? Even if these performances draw on established tropes, their performances are always temporary, and each time they are performed they are different. The nation and culture, then, are not just always in motion but also in performance. If nothing else, these self-exoticising spectacles are also part of cultural diplomacy, an area of museum practice that has received too little scholarly attention.

A third project that is relevant here did not take place at the Weltmuseum Wien but was an art project by the Brazilian artist Ernesto Neto in which he involved the Amazonian Huni Kuin peoples. The project was hosted by TB21, the Thyssen Bornemisza Art Contemporary, in 2015. This example not only resonates with ethnographic museum collaborations with Amazonian peoples, but also reveals some of the pitfalls of such formats of inclusion that equally affect frontline contemporary art institutions that try to adopt reflexive practices.

TB21 is a private foundation and at the time operated an exhibition space in Vienna dedicated primarily to the commissioning and dissemination of ambitious, experimental, and nonconventional art projects that defy traditional categorisation and that are often informed by an interest in social aesthetics and environmental concerns. Neto is known for installations that transcend boundaries of physical and social space through interactive, tactile, and biomorphic structures that engage viewers in a sensory experience. TB21 contacted the Weltmuseum Wien to collaborate in jointly hosting visiting representatives of the Huni Kuin who had come to Vienna for Neto's exhibition, welcoming them to the museum, and giving them access to and therefore understanding of the museum's Amazonian collections.

In June of 2015, The TB21 announced 'Aru Kuxipa | Sacred Secret' as follows:

> Aru Kuxipa, conceived as Ernesto Neto's personal tribute to the Huni Kuin, unfolds as a subtle parcours, which transitions from a space of preparation and initiation to the sacred area of ritual, to a room of study and knowledge, culminating in the community's multiple voices of myths and songs. Neto mobilizes a deep understanding of indigenous wisdom and tradition and the relational and perspectival nature of the Huni Kuin's world vision. This shared journey marks a crucial extension of concerns that have been evident in his oeuvre over the past twenty years: an appreciation of the sensuality of being, the unity of bodies and nature, the celebration of life, and a search for deeper forms of union and correspondence.[3]

In addition to honouring the Huni Kuin, the exhibition also focused on the *Book of Healing*, the first compilation of descriptions of the 109 plant species used by the Huni Kuin and their applications in various curative treatments. The project

---

[3] From the TB21 press release of 25 June 2015: http://press.tba21.org/News_Detail.aspx?id=45023&menueid=9361.

also included a residency for seven young Huni Kuin leaders, which was considered a dynamic part of the exhibition aiming at 'engaging in novel encounters and opening the stage to new inquiries and challenges pressing specifically its younger generation at present'[4]. As part of their residency, these young leaders gave talks about their traditional hunting, fishing, and agricultural practices, and the exhibition's programme further included a body-painting workshop, food presentation, a symposium on natural healing practices in Austria and the Amazon, lectures on environmental and indigenous rights issues, and art conversations with Neto and the Huni Kuin.

At the opening, held at TB21, an art crowd assembled in the stunning ambience of Neto's artistic interpretation of a Huni Kuin assembly house, all sitting in a circle listening to Neto's introductory remarks. In the presence of Huni Kuin representatives, Neto spoke of them as 'these people' and 'they'; only later did he introduce some of them by name. He underscored their close connection to nature, speaking about the medicines the Huni Kuin derive from plants and their 'traditional wisdom'. Neto stated: 'The sacred knowledge is from this planet earth, which is suffering so much from the actions of this period', and 'They are here, they have the healing, and they have a lot to teach'.

Neto also referred to the songs of the Huni Kuin and drawings made as part of the project, saying: 'There is no separation between life and art', the future lies in the 'Homo artisticus', and, in a conjuring voice: 'They are like in the future, [they have] a very healthy relation with life and nature'. Referring to the space created in the gallery, Neto proclaimed, 'We are here to create a zone of contact', which should enable social encounters between people.

In her speech, Francesca Habsburg, the president of the TB21 foundation, thanked the Huni Kuin for her having been able to absorb all of their love and happiness when she visited them in Brazil, when she spent three days and three nights in their 'extraordinary' culture. The collaboration, she said, 'helps us to deepen our respect for our environment'. Habsburg then asked the group for a small ceremony or a song to celebrate the birthday of an acquaintance of hers that was present at the opening.

The collaboration had been discussed in Brazil with the community and the Huni Kuin had agreed to participate because they felt that their culture was valued in Europe while they faced discrimination in their own country. Even though there was respect and interest from the public, their presence became a spectacle in which the longing for the exotic played a central role and they ended up being framed, however unintentionally, as 'noble savages'. The sincere intentions of the curators who tried to make the experience for the Huni Kuin rewarding, and to do so in a respectful way, became entangled in a presentation of the group as idealised

---

4   Ibidem.

'people of nature'. This framing resonates with academic debates in which groups are idealised as 'ecologically noble savages', who live in harmony with nature; this conception confines people into a 'repressive authenticity' to live up to stereotypical imaginations of an ecological nobility (Rowland 2004; Nadasdy 2005).

The way Huni Kuin representatives were addressed in these introductory remarks, particularly in the use of 'they' by Neto, was reminiscent of colonial narratives in which, as Marie Louise Pratt (1985, 120) explains, 'the people to be othered are homogenised into a collective "they"'. This long tradition has been, and sometimes still is, a common practice characteristic for holocultural representational modes in ethnographic contexts.

By way of comparison it might be enlightening to look back to a historic example of exhibiting peoples: Hilke Thode-Arora (2014) has presented her archival research and fieldwork on the history of Samoan ethnic shows in Europe, which resulted in an exhibition and her book *From Samoa with Love: Samoan Travelers in Germany 1895-1911, Retracing the Footsteps*. Her work clearly shows that that the Samoan participants in these shows were self-determined actors and not victims. Looking at three such traveling shows, which were organised by the German brothers Fritz and Carl Marquardt in 1895-97, 1900/01 and 1910/11, Thode-Arora details who participated, where the performances took place, and what happened among the participants, including personal stories and the politics in Samoa and Germany surrounding them. She explains that the participants, most of whom came from high-ranking families in Samoa, opted themselves to go on this trip, and that most of them were able to build on the symbolic capital of having visited Germany after their return to Samoa.

After mishaps during the first tour, resulting from a lack of respect for social hierarchies among the participants, a high-ranking Samoan member of society was hired to coordinate and lead the group and to choose its members for the second and third tours. On the third tour a contender for the Samoan throne, Tupua Tamasese Lealofi, was selected for this role, whose absence from Samoa was deemed helpful for the local political climate by the German colonial administration. Tamasese himself wanted to take this trip, which he saw in the Samoan tradition of a 'malaga', a diplomatic visit in which a chief and his followers would visit another village, where he would be treated royally. He also planned to meet with nobility, the emperor, and other powerful men in Germany. Thode-Arora writes that Tamasese had come to Germany with the assumption of going on a diplomatic tour and complained about being exhibited in front of people in zoos. In the end, it was made possible for him to meet the German emperor and to have encounters with prominent German businessmen. According to Thode-Arora, remembrance of the 'trips' and the associated prestige is still alive among the participants' descendants.

It is necessary to point out that this is one particular story, similar to some others but also different from many other stories. In the history of such human shows, people often were forced to participate, many died because of illnesses or mistreatment, and they were coerced to conform to stereotypical expectations (Blanchard, Boetsch, and Jacomjin Snoep 2011). As Laura Peers (2007) points out, in the late nineteenth century American Indians also took part in cultural performance groups, often because they offered good income opportunities and possibilities to travel. The performances allowed the participants to communicate information about their cultures to foreign audiences, to express pride in their heritage and traditions, and to use stereotyped images of themselves for their own purposes. But should we interpret or foreground these stories as practices of agency, in relation to other stories of domination and oppression? If we foreground the positive aspects, what does it mean for how we understand colonial oppression? There is a need to apply caution against presenting these as happy narratives or forwarding too-simplistic ideas of agency under colonialism. Yet, I find they are also useful to bring attention to practices of self-representation.

All the mentioned groups – the Samoans, the Huni Kuin, and the Bon priests – proudly presented and enacted their culture under the gaze of European spectators; the same holds true for the Nigerian association in Austria. Can we compare these contemporary practices with the historic example of the Samoans during the colonial period? According to Peers, who compared past cultural performances like the Buffalo Bill performers with contemporary American Indian interpreters at historic sites, the major difference is that the latter communicate messages they themselves determine, while the stagings in the past supported a dominant-society version of history. Peers (2007, 64) writes: 'The dynamics of such performances differ greatly from those expressed by Buffalo Bill's Native performers, who also "played themselves", but in shows in which their image, actions and messages were controlled by Cody to support a dominant-society version of history. This is not the case for the Native interpreters at historic sites today who communicate messages that they themselves determine, in addition to the official themes of the sites, and who use their work to pursue their own agendas'. Peers underscores that cultural performances can be both a way of oppression and a way of resisting authority. A unidimensional reading of cultural performers would suggest passivity, lack of agency, and victimisation. But does the historic site and the narrative it promotes – as a frame for the interactions of the American Indian performers – impact the audience's perception?

In all the examples described, encounters played a central role. Thode-Arora acknowledges that in addition to the voyeuristic, patronising attitude of the viewers of human shows in the late nineteenth and early twentieth century, there seemingly was an 'overwhelming need' among the spectators to communicate and interact with the performers. Such encounters are today usually considered to foster increased respect and understanding between peoples. Can we assume it was the case also in the past? Is this really the case today?

In all examples the participating communities followed a strategy and had a clear agenda. The Bon priests wanted to give their little-known religion more presence in Europe and raise funds to repair their monastery building. The Nigerian Austrian association wanted to convey a positive image of their community in Austria, where Nigerians are often associated with drug dealings or illegal prostitution, to further integration and conviviality and claim a presence in Austrian society. The Huni Kuin delegation used their residency in Austria to advocate for the respect of their traditions and sovereignty in Brazil and to denounce threats to their environment. The Samoans gained not only social capital after their return, due to their world experience, but also strategic advantage because of their first-hand insight into the culture and politics in Germany, the colonial power that controlled their homeland.

All groups had their own objectives determining why they engaged in the interactions, framed by a strategic deployment of essentialist notions of their culture, and they used the public moment for their own empowerment in different ways. Even if going along with self-exoticisation might be an acceptable path to advance these communities' agendas, adopting strategic essentialism certainly would be questionable if dictated by the hosting institutions. Most ethnographic museums have distanced themselves from practices that essentialise cultures and lead to stereotypical images. Is it acceptable then for this to happen in an ethnographic museum, or does this backdrop affect such strategies unintentionally? What should be the museum's role: to enable such public performances, to interpret them, to mediate, or to curate, taking charge and responsibility? Who should have the authority to control what happens?

Are some, to our view possibly exotic, performances only projections of what the actors feel is expected from them in this environment or is it a self-determined representation of their own culture? How can the museum manage or minimise the voyeuristic longing of their audiences for the exotic?

Despite all shortcomings and the ambivalence of exoticisation or self-exoticisation in the process, the events described were accompanied by community members' feelings of pride in their cultural heritage and a gratitude to the museum for giving space to these spectacles that affirmed sovereignty and self-determination.

So, did Kravagna's critique of collaborations and associated cultural events as colonial have a point? Or was it a misunderstanding of self-determined representations within the context of ethnographic museums? In either case, how can we better frame folkloric performances, which often are self-empowering moments not only for diasporic communities?

To answer many of the questions I have posed here, we need more research on how such events are received. We also might need to air our reservations about such practices openly and discuss them with the participants themselves, to jointly seek better ways to frame and choreograph such events.

And, finally, how can we deal with this ambivalence: while we harbour an aversion against proliferating nationalist, ethnic, essentialist and folkloric expressions in our own society in its present shift to the right, we on the other hand tend to be supportive when the production of difference is a strategy by diasporic communities to claim their right of belonging? If anything, these observations should invite us to engage in theoretical discussions on the right to culture and self-determination, on nation branding and cultural diplomacy, and on issues related to the strategic mobilisation of tropes of the 'ecological noble savage', they should invite us to thinking about the relationship between what happens in and outside the walls of ethnographic museums.

## References

Bennett, Tony. 1995. *The Birth of the Museum: History, Theory, Politics.* London: Routledge.

Blanchard, Pascal, Gilles Boetsch, and Nanette Jacomjin Snoep, eds. 2011. *Human Zoos: The Invention of the Savage.* Paris: Musée du quai Branly and Actes Sud.

Guss, David M. 2000. *The Festive State: Race, Ethnicity, and Nationalism as Cultural Performance.* Berkeley: University of California Press.

Hooper, Steven, Karen Jacobs, Maja Jessup, and George Nuku. 2012. 'Encounters with Polynesia in Britain: Art, Ancestors, Artists, and Curators'. *Museum Anthropology* 35, no. 1: 10-22.

Klimburg-Salter, Deborah, Linda Lojda, and Charles Ramble, eds. 2013. *BÖN: Spirits in Butter. Art and Ritual of Old Tibet.* Vienna: Museum für Völkerkunde. https://www.univie.ac.at/boen_geisterausbutter/wp-content/uploads/2013/04/bon_geisterausbutter.pdf.

Kravagna, Christian. 2015. 'Vom ethnologischen Museum zum unmöglichen Kolonialmuseum'. *Zeitschrift für Kulturwissenschaften* 1: 95-100.

Mathur, Saloni, and Kavita Singh. 2017. 'Reincarnations of the Museum: The Museum in an Age of Religious Revivalism'. In *No Touching, No Spitting, No Praying: The Museum in South Asia*, edited by Saloni Mathur and Kavita Singh, 149. New Delhi: Routledge India.

Nadasdy, Paul. 2005. 'Transcending the Debate over the Ecologically Noble Indian: Indigenous Peoples and Environmentalism'. *Ethnohistory* 52, no. 2: 292-331.

Peers, Laura. 2007. *Playing Ourselves: Interpreting Native Histories at Historic Reconstructions.* Lanham, MD: Altamira Press.

Plankensteiner, Barbara. 2015. 'Beherrscht die Sammlung uns oder wir die Sammlung? Eine Replik auf Christian Kravagna aus dem Inneren des ethnographischen Museums'. *Zeitschrift für Kulturwissenschaften* 1: 105-7.

Pratt, Mary Louise. 2007. *Imperial Eyes: Travel Writing and Transculturation*. London, New York: Routledge.

Rowland, Michael J. 2004. 'Return of the "Noble Savage": Misrepresenting the Past, Present and Future'. *Australian Aboriginal Studies* 2: 2-14.

Thode-Arora, Hilke, ed. 2014. *From Samoa with Love? Samoan Travelers in Germany 1895-1911: Retracing the Footsteps.* Munich: Hirmer Verlag.

Fig. 4.1. 'Untitled'. Author: Makamo. Sandalwood. Mozambique. Collection: Aurnhammer. Entry date: 1989. Inv. F 54286. Copyright Linden-Museum Stuttgart. Photo: Anatol Dryer.

# Our House Is Made of Thin, Burning Ice. Let's Dance

SANDRA FERRACUTI

*Eu acho que há muita coisa que sonhamos em comun.*
I believe that we have many dreams in common.

- Malangatana Ngwenya in Noronha 2007

The roots of this paper lie in the exchanges I had with the critical and engaged participants of two European projects: 'Ethnography Museums and World Cultures' (RIME, 2008-2013) and 'Réseau Européen des Associations de Diasporas et Musées Ethnographiques' (READ-ME, 2007-2012).[1] During that time, I was, together with Rosa Anna di Lella and Elisabetta Frasca, assisting Vito Lattanzi, as a member of the Pigorini Museum's team, which was based in Rome, the city where I was born and lived.[2]

This chapter addresses the same 'family of themes' as the 'Sharing a World of Inclusion, Creativity, and Heritage' (SWICH) project – the latest iteration of the series of European projects mentioned above – which from 2014 to 2018 has focused on the predicament and possible futures of ethnography museums in Europe. And while it is also directly connected to my current participation in that project, it is written from quite a different standpoint.

## Journeys

I am an Italian citizen, now 'playing' with the German museum team. Since January 2016, I have a job, a home address, and a public health insurance provider in Stuttgart. The Linden-Museum has entrusted me with the care of its collections from Africa, and so I immigrated to Germany for work, just like many other Italians before me,[3] also in search of job opportunities. And here I am, where many peope who live in precarity just south of Sicily (in Lybia, for example) are also most probably trying to move as I write these very words, but at much too great a risk to their lives.

In 2016 my position in the field of the anthropology of heritages and museums changed significantly. Before then, I had mainly been engaged in scholarly research *about* museums and heritage; now I am *acting from within* them.[4] The Linden-Museum in Stuttgart gave me the opportunity to make a decisive shift towards a more applied approach. Believing as I do that it is crucial that we increase reflexive

---

1  On these projects, see, among others, Bouttiaux and Seiderer (2011), Munapé (2012), and Ferracuti, Frasca, and Lattanzi (2013).
2  At that time, Lattanzi was head of the Ethnography Department at the Museo Nazionale Preistorico Etnografico 'Luigi Pigorini' (now merged into the Museo delle Civiltà) and coordinated the participation of the Italian museum in these European projects.
3  There is a long history of migration from Italy to Germany, especially for work. This is a practice that is still ongoing.
4  An important exception was the opportunity I had between 2004 and 2005 to work as curator at the Fondazione Museo Ettore Guatelli, directed by Mario Turci.

and critical contemporary anthropological approaches in the work of public institutions, and perhaps with a certain degree of recklessness, I accepted the challenge of working, in such delicate and uncertain times[5], on a project to renovate this German museum's permanent exhibition of African collections.

Even if the period of official German occupation of African territories was relatively brief (1884-1919), it was during this time that the vast majority of the Linden-Museum's collection of approximately forty thousand artefacts from the African continent was acquired by soldiers, colonial administrators, entrepreneurs, missionaries, collectors, and dealers. For later acquisitions, at least until decolonisation took place across the African continent, leading to the birth of independent African states at the end of the 1950s, dealers and collectors, such as those who were in contact with the Württembergischen Vereins für Handelsgeographie,[6] could still count on networks of European actors whose acquisition, transport, and exchange of artefacts across the world were facilitated by existing colonial structures.[7] Indeed, some scholars have argued that these structures still remain intact even today with a decolonisation process that is yet to achieve its goals.

My approach to the renovation, then, has been informed by this history, and by a deep awareness of the delicate nature of this kind of museum work in what could be described as the unfinished colonial moment. It has also benefitted from an engagement with the museological innovations around questions of inclusion that have taken place in recent decades, including within the three European Union-funded projects I referred to above. Over the past three years, while developing the concept for a new exhibition, I have been thinking of and experimenting with possible platforms through which to do 'collaborative' or 'participatory' activities with different stakeholders. This was with a view to enabling the museum, a public institution, to engage in a steady exchange with Stuttgart's plural citizenry, of whom almost half are of migrant background. One of the main platforms with whom I have worked has been the Advisory Board for the Representation of African Collections (ABRAC), a group comprising vibrant civil society actors who moved to Germany from different African countries. I take these efforts to engage

---

5   Here I refer not just to the current moment of political anxiety across the world, but also to contemporary questions surrounding the present and future of ethnographic museums and their collections.
6   The Württemberg´s Association for Commercial Geography, to which the Linden-Museum owes its foundation and early life, was founded in 1882 and chaired by Karl Graf von Linden from 1887 until his death in 1910. The museum became a public institution, owned in partnership by the Baden-Württemberg Land and the City of Stuttgart, only in 1973.
7   The uneven power relations established during the colonial period still inform global inequalities. It is for this reason that it is healthy to consider our own collecting contexts in this light, as was recently done by Claudia Augustat in the permanent exhibition of the Weltmuseum Wien, where she questioned the structure of power within which she herself acquired an object for the museum collection some years ago.

stakeholders as part of the right of 'heritage communities' to act within public spaces that are devoted, as the Faro Convention states, to interpreting 'the value of cultural heritage for society' (Council of Europe 2005) and as spaces in which to creatively 'perform citizenship' (Isin 2017).

The Faro Convention[8] frames cultural heritage within the broader scope of human rights, which are at the core of the Council of Europe's mission. The convention also endorses democratic participation within the public heritage system. It defines cultural heritage as 'a group of resources inherited from the past which people identify, *independently of ownership*, as a reflection and expression of their constantly evolving values, beliefs, knowledge and traditions' (Art. 2(a); emphasis added). The definition of 'heritage community' – '*people who value specific aspects of cultural heritage* which they wish, within the framework of public action, to *sustain and transmit to future generations*' (Art. 2(b); emphasis added) – is based on the idea that, beyond commonly recognised heritage actors such as public officials and legislators, other groups participate in heritage politics, starting from the very identification of what should constitute cultural heritage.

The German state has not ratified the Faro Convention. Still, I consider the main group of people I have been working among at the Linden-Museum as a 'heritage community'. In this sense I believe that we are acting in a way that resonates with Engin Isin's (2017) concept of 'performative citizenship', where steps are taken that might provoke a change in how specific heritage goods are claimed as rights, or cared for, or taken as one's responsibility. Our 'house' is burning: let's dance in it.

The members of ABRAC as heritage community are among the residents of Baden-Württemberg who are most impacted by the enduring effects of Eurocentrism, racism, and primitivizing narratives. These narratives have served as 'theoretical' grounds for the violent, exploitative relationship of many parts of the world to Africa, and for the negative representations of the African continent. Within these narratives *Völkerkunde* museums have been complicit. These narratives, constructed and propagated as imperialistic tools, turn African bodies into battlefields, struck from both the inside and the outside. It is from within this space of embattlement that ABRAC members are actively engaged in advocating for a society that allows them and their children to feel at home.

Throughout the project my aim has been to enhance the opportunities offered by the museological and museographical application of the ethnographic method, and here I mean an effort to *listen and translate* within the museum context. Moreover, I want to optimise reflexive and dialogic perspectives that facilitate thinking in the terms of an *'Us' in the here and now*, where 'Us' is the people of

---

8   The full text of the convention can be accessed here: https://www.coe.int/en/web/conventions/full-list/-/conventions/rms/0900001680083746. For interpretive views on this legislation, see also Ferracuti (2009) and Zagato and Vecco (2011).

Baden-Württemberg seen as perfectly able to love more than one place and dream in more than one language.

These aims are grounded in the belief that, while it is widely recognised that the discipline of anthropology played a role in creating and bolstering Eurocentric, even racist paradigms in the past, the discipline's more recent practices may well be among the most useful to combat these same issues, especially in the framework of European ethnography museums. I believe that the long-lasting detachment between academic anthropology and museum anthropology has until recently contributed not only to the sustaining of 'old-fashioned' ethnographic representations but also to reducing the relevance that critical anthropology can have in today's societies.

## 'My Africa'

> Linking the living, the dead, and those to come as a continuous community, we become responsible for the past in its entirety. Informed tolerance toward our total legacy is a necessary condition of enhancing the present and enabling the future.
> - *The Past is a Foreign Country - Revisited*, David Lowenthal, Cambridge University Press, 2015 (quote from Introduction, page 22)

Up until 2016, my research focused on Mozambique and in particular its capital city Maputo, where most of my explorations concerned the transnational 'art-culture systems' (Clifford 1988, 224) active in the country between 2005 and 2010.

Since living in Stuttgart, as an Italian responsible for a German collection of African artefacts, my own sense of belonging has increasingly come into question. The feeling of estrangement that I have experienced here is much deeper than in any other place where I have lived previously, and it has led me to consider whether being born in Rome and now living in Stuttgart confers any true sense of being 'Italian' or 'European', whether I really belonged to Europe. The day before my job interview at the Linden-Museum, I realised that its permanent exhibition included a work by Mozambican sculptor Samson Makamo (born 1945). I met Makamo in 2010 in Maputo, where he lives and works, and my exchanges with him greatly contributed to my gaining access to the wide, complex, and stratified vision of the world that he shares with many of his fellow citizens (see Ferracuti 2016).

It is quite unusual to encounter works by living artists in the permanent galleries of European ethnographic museums (especially works that date back to the 1980s) and Mozambique is not a significantly relevant region for the Linden's African collection. Hence my surprise. The importance that I ascribe to this unexpected encounter derives from the fact that Makamo's philosophical vision has be-

Fig. 4.2. The 'Oku Palace' installation in 2016, Linden-Museum´s 'Africa' Hall. Copyright Linden-Museum Stuttgart. Photo: Dominik Drasdow.

come part of my own. His sculpture in Stuttgart is a familiar presence in a strange land, a presence so meaningful that it made me feel that there could actually be a good reason for me to be there. I am reminded of a comment (recounted to me by a colleague) made by the scholar Sibe Grovogui, that perhaps the problem with having objects from other parts of the world in Europe is not only about issues of ownership or restitution, but also that we have never allowed these objects to disturb our sense of ourselves, to impact our philosophy of the world. These objects have for too long been presented as how others are, and not as how we could be[9].

Makamo is not only an artist of rightful fame, whose most relevant works are exhibited in Maputo's Museu Nacional de Arte. He is also a healer, a *curandeiro* with the ability to reach and interact with a powerful world of 'deities' who share their secrets with him, and with the spirit world of the dead who, from the afterworld not seen by most, weave connections among the living. Makamo explained to me that our dialogue would not conclude at our passing from life. In fact, any possible conflicts between us, if left unresolved, would continue to irritate us in the afterlife and the weight of their burden would eventually fall on the heads of our descendants.

Makamo's idea of the afterworld puts everyone in the same dimension of reality; it brings us closer together: the near, the far, the living, the dead, the yet-to-be-born. He explained: if conflicts were to develop between us and remain unresolved, even if distance allowed us not to face the consequences of these conflicts during our lives, our descendants would not be able to find a safe distance from our restless spirits, even if we died far away from each other, me in Rome and he in Maputo.

Since meeting Makamo, I have often thought of our postcolonial Euro-African relations in these terms. Makamo's view resonates with me now, with the vision expressed by David Lowenthal in the epigraph; their voices blend in my head, coming together with others who had an impact on me long before them. They lead me to ask: can facing up to and recognising the impact of colonial violence appease our ancestors? Might the museum as a 'temple' be a good place in which to experience shared rituals that, as Lowenthal (22) writes, 'enhanc[e] the present and enabl[e] the future'?

Makamo's work at the Linden-Museum has woven threads of familiarity between me and a city quite indifferent to me. Stuttgart was alien to my presence, unknowing of my personal experience. Makamo's vision ultimately allowed me to unite our destinies and gave heartfelt meaning to my being in the museum. Hopefully, more citizens of Stuttgart will be able to feel at home within its walls. This can only happen, however, if the museum can forge a narrative of identity

---

9    I would like to thank Wayne Modest for bringing this to my attention. In fact, this is also what Valentin-Yves Mudimbe meant with his concept of 'epistemological ethnocentrism' (1988).

that is multiplex, one that is capable of giving a glimpse into how human beings shape each other across political, social, and geographical borders, and into how they contribute to shaping the world.

My interview on the following day went well. And here I am, sharing the prospects and goals that are guiding my reflections towards a new permanent exhibition in Stuttgart. Certainly, it is not an easy task, also because the past display (even if visually dated) reflected the competence and critical approach of my predecessors, Hans-Joachim Koloss (from 1973 through 1985) and Hermann Forkl (from 1986 through 2014). The past display made visible the historical depth of the wide circulation of people, objects, and ideas that characterise the African continent, as well as the impact of colonial violence on its peoples, their dignity, and their resources. Furthermore, it also accounted for the contemporary political, cultural, and economic relations between Europe and Africa, which one can hardly define as 'balanced' or equal.

## Africa in Stuttgart: Reflexive Ethnographic Research with a View to an Exhibition

*Bien venu chez vous chez nous, car chez nous vous êtes chez vous.*
Welcome to us at your place, because at our place you are at home.
- Stone Karim Mohamad, unpublished poem, 2016

In my exhibition design, I have drawn on the expertise that twenty years of anthropological training in reflexive ethnographic research have given me. The Italian school of museum anthropology to which I belong, the Società Italiana per la Museografia e i Beni Demoetnoantropologici (Italian Society for Museum and Heritage Anthropology, Simbdea), insists on this as a key tool for good practice. Similarly, in the United States, where my training began in the early nineties, reflexivity was the basic building block of the trade of cultural anthropologists. These two traditions underpin my habitus, guiding me to look at cultural heritage as the result of contingent processes of meaning attribution, as the result of the specific structures of the here and now. They are cultural, social, political, and economic contingencies in which the legacies of the past always play a role.

The past and present social life of the African cultural heritage preserved at the Linden-Museum is what I have chosen as the main subject for research in developing the new display. Although I have tried to take every opportunity presented to me to continue exploring African local contexts, my intention is not to make 'Africa' the singular or main focus of the exhibition. Rather, I intend to focus 'in house' and, taking advantage of my own 'outsider's' perspective, explore the spaces existing between the museum collections and different groups of past and present local actors. My aim is to include some hints of their (both actual and imaginary) relationships with the museum's collections.

Within this framework, my own experiences and reflections on how identity is defined in relation to nationality are put in the service of the design of the exhibition. The narrative of 'national cultural identity' is widely taken for 'the norm', but what if transnational cultural flows, relationships, and encounters actually were more relevant to the human experience? In so-called multicultural societies, isn't it more relevant to focus on, and display, interconnections and multiplexity as inherent to them and enriching rather than as some kind of 'exception' to 'tolerate'?

A first group of actors whose relationships with the collection I have been exploring consists of my predecessors, curators at the Linden-Museum. In addition, I am interested in the numerous students, scholars, researchers, artists, activists, amateurs, and collectors who get in touch with me almost on a daily basis to ask about the department's interest in acquiring objects and collections, or to obtain information on specific artefacts, or to consult documentation associated with donations made to the museum by one of their ancestors. There are also those who wish to further historical, artistic or ethnographic study in which they are involved, to request loans, to develop artistic projects related to the African continent, or to raise postcolonial questions. These contacts give me access to the diversity of the local 'passions' for Africa, and visions and concerns as expressed today within Europe.

The second group of 'accomplices' (Marcus 1997) in my research process are museum professionals, scholars, and artists based in African countries who are also interrogating the continent's cultural resources, the histories and legacies of colonialism that European collections embody, and their potentialities for the future.

My most stable research partners, however, are the members of the 'African diaspora' who make up the ABRAC, which was officially inaugurated in July 2016 with the support of Inés de Castro, the director of the Linden-Museum. It is based on the model developed by the African Associations Committee, which since 2003 has been in dialogue with Royal Museum for Central Africa in Tervuren, Belgium. The ten members of the ABRAC[10] periodically join me in exploring priorities, opinions, and goals associated with the representation of the African continent's cultural heritage in Stuttgart. I was able to get in touch with them thanks to the mediation of Sara Alterio, who works at the Forum der Kulturen in Stuttgart, an umbrella organisation founded in 1989 to which at least one hundred associations align themselves in committing to spreading knowledge about the important lega-

---

10   Olimpio Alberto, Steve Loic Lefang, Afonso Manguele, Stone Karim Mohamad, Pierre Bayangane Mpama, Djenneba Obot, Ekarika Nanna Obot, Natacha Tschoumi Pettie, Cathy Nzimbu Mpanu-Mpanu-Plato, and Felix Abayomi Saka.

cies that immigrants carry with them. Among these, about thirty are composed of members of the 'African diaspora'.

The members of the ABRAC were selected by me based on a specific set of criteria. The first criteria guiding the selection of possible members was 'geographical': I worked to make contact with German residents who were born in Cameroon, the Congo River basin, Nigeria, and Mozambique. The first three of these regions coincided with the areas where the largest numbers of objects in the museum collections from Africa came from, and have been the focus of much of the research and installations of the curators who preceded me. The choice to add Mozambican members to the group was based on my own experience.[11]

A second guiding principle of the selection process was the availability and interest of my interlocutors to be in dialogue with me on the past, present, and future of the museum's African collections. And that availability is not to be taken for granted, given the already very active professional and social engagements of these members of civil society and the controversial, postcolonial nature of European ethnographic institutions. With these two criteria in mind, I also chose to acknowledge and allow for processes of serendipity. This meant that I could take advantage of the good fortune I had in meeting people who were already pursuing goals (with passion, tenacity, and courage) that just so happened to be similar to mine – from a personal and professional point of view – and to those that the Linden-Museum has set for its own mission. My first encounter with Stone Karim Mohamad, for example, a member of the ABRAC and a Cameroonian citizen[12] who had been living in Germany for some years, became an important source of motivation for me. When he was first introduced to me in 2016 by Steve Lefang, the president of the 'Eyes on Cameroon' organization based in Gäufelden (Baden-Württemberg, Germany), Mohamad openly stated his quite critical view on ethnographic museums in European cities. After he shared his scepticism with me, I shared my own view on the matter: 'I think there are two things that we can do now: 1) close everything or 2) try to turn it upside down'. 'Let's give it a try', he said. And that is what we have been doing.

## Where Is Africa? Or, of a Deafening Silence

'*Migration macht krank*' (migration makes you sick) was uttered unapologetically by one of my German language teachers, and a large and growing number of the present inhabitants of Stuttgart actually live this condition. Who knows, however, whether such a positioning in the world does not also stimulate creativity, allowing

---

11   It would also be quite difficult to deny that this choice also resides in a personal longing for feeling 'at home' on my part.
12   Cameroon does not allow for dual citizenship.

us to imagine new ways to reside and cohabit? Many 'diasporic' individuals have actually dedicated themselves to what has been called 'arts of the diaspora' or 'arts of migration' (Cafuri 2005): artistic practices that may also underpin a search for companionship, alliances, or a sense of belonging, including a quest for citizenship.

It is well-known what is happening along the southern borders of Europe. Arguably, as 'an Italian' I understand these issues more deeply, being born in a country with borders in the south at Lampedusa and in the north at Ventimiglia and the Brenner Pass. Now having been given the opportunity to work in a European public institution that participates in the education of citizens, I also have the opportunity to participate in the construction of contexts that facilitate the feeling of being at home. Museums could help to create narratives of citizenship based on more inclusive forms of membership.

I argue that, in museological terms, the new exhibition, 'Wo ist Afrika?' (Where is Africa?'), should contribute to three main goals. The first is to inform visitors that the historical collections are rooted in nineteenth-century European attitudes and in colonial violence, while allowing these collections to also act as testimonies to the heritage of the African continent, whose global relevance is undeniable. My second goal is to provide German citizens of African origin with a sense of pride in a collection that they feel a sense of ownership of and, using the terms of the Faro Convention, that 'they wish, within the framework of public action, to sustain and transmit to future generations'. The third goal aims to challenge visitors to reflect upon, get involved in, and exchange questions, whether trivial or provocative, such as: what do I know about the African continent? What does it mean to be African? What does it mean to be European? What vision do I have of the continent and its inhabitants? How was it shaped? Have I ever been to an African country? What did I learn? The way I see it, it is time to engage in the study of a wider history, activate reflexive processes, and share questions that affect us all as active agents of our times and co-builders of a shared future.

The word 'Africa' conjures vivid images. But even though European countries had occupied 90 per cent of the African continent by 1900, the histories, languages (some 1,500), and cultural legacies of this extremely culturally diverse continent are virtually absent from most educational curricula around the world. This results in the misrepresentation of the continent, or its obscuring, by many. Paradoxically, much is projected onto 'Africa' through centuries of Eurocentric narratives, with even the word itself evoking vivid and intense images in the minds of many. Still, how much do we actually *know*? Visions of a land of 'simple, untamed, wild-natured, primitive, dangerous, mysterious, instinctive peoples' still haunt Eurocentric narratives about Africa, and thus hinder the view of an entire continent. These imaginations are a legacy of the many narratives – disguised as objective 'science' (racist theories), models of 'civilisation' (unilinear evolutionism, which organised human societies from 'primitive' to 'civilised'), notions of 'modernity', and 'evangelisation' (the global expansion of monotheisms) -that drowned curiosity in judgment. These visions still blind many. We have lost much in terms of human creativity, due to what Congolese philosopher Valentin-Yves Mudimbe (1988, 28) has termed 'epistemological ethnocentrism', meaning 'the belief that scientifically there is nothing to be learned from "them" unless it is already "ours" or comes from us'. Perhaps we need to take time, a special quality of time, to learn to listen to some of the many stories that we have not yet been (cap)able of hearing. Perhaps ethnographic museums can play a role in this.

## Karingana wa karingana

In southern Mozambique, the phrase *'karingana wa karingana'* is uttered to make those present aware that a special time to listen has come. When it is pronounced, everyone turns silent: an important story is about to be told, one that has a *long breath*, over time and space, one that is about us. Museums have their own 'long breath': they are special places where sharing stories can also be a form of poetry, a way to tell ourselves new stories, and a means to imagine all that we can be.

With a view toward switching our gazes from 'them, there', to 'us, here' and contributing to dispelling the vision of imaginary, faraway 'Others', the new exhibition will hopefully contribute to sharing with visitors a broader understanding of 'us' here and now. This will involve inviting visitors to challenge assumptions with curiosity, to listen to and reflect on their own experiences (actual and imagined) of the themes presented the exhibition, and to consider their perception of and actual interactions with African heritages, so as to enrich their very notion of 'us' by focusing on historical and present entanglements, relationships, connections, and exchanges, both actual and potential. 'Africa' and its tangible and intangible heritages are culturally, politically, economically, socially, spiritually 'here' too, and they have always been.

It is my hope that this exhibit will convey a contemporary understanding of the anthropological concept of culture, where worldviews are constantly negotiated, tradition is a dynamic process based on cultural creativity, and individuals are more than 'representatives' of reductive and often arbitrary 'ethnic', national, geographical, generational, political, or social affiliations. Instead, individuals will be cast as both permeable and active agents within political, natural, moral, and economic environments, the ones they are raised in, those they settle in, the ones they communicate and interact with, and the ones they traverse throughout their lives, all of which they both interpret and help to transform. It is in such complex and restless fluidity where change and continuity, belonging to and diverging from, defining and subverting, believing and doubting, knowing and wishing all dynamically coexist that, perhaps, the 'authentic' nature of the human species is to be found.

And that includes museum curators. It is for this reason that I have chosen to let reflexivity (the open acknowledgement of how the biography and *habitus* of collectors, researchers, and educators, and the structures of their interactions inevitably contribute to shape their work) enter this essay as well as the exhibition, and to share with our visitors some narratives and points of view about past and present relationships that artefacts in our Africa collection are testimonies to, products of, and/or means towards.

From such a perspective, the exhibition should offer glimpses both into the kind of contexts within which the African artefacts on display were originally performed, and into the global, transcultural, and relational qualities of the histories and movements that are linked to the development and display of this kind of collection. Objects can shed light on the subjectivities and the relationships that have brought these objects to life, and on how human beings can be creatively and meaningfully different while being the same, across time and space.

An assertive, monological narrative would limit our actual possibility to interrogate and enjoy the complexity and the essentially relational nature of the human cultural experience. For this reason, I have chosen to give space to storytelling and share with visitors the points of views and understandings of some of those who have contributed and still contribute to both *share* knowledges and *co-construct* visions of 'Africa', within and without the museum. Hopefully, by including in the display the actual relationships that have produced the collections and the encounters that artefacts have witnessed or even made possible will contribute to making them more available to the current public discourse on 'us', making clear that interconnections are not an 'exception' but instead at the heart of museum collections themselves.

∗

## Sharing the Ride

> *Sortirne tutti insieme è la politica. Sortirne da soli è l'avarizia.*
> To find a way out all together is politics. To find a way out alone is greed.
> - Lorenzo Milani, *Lettera a una professoressa* (Letter to a Professor), 1967.

The experiments in dialogue with members of Stuttgart's civil society are not *geared towards* the opening of an exhibition. Our relationships will hopefully lead to a 'visible outcome', but the more I engage in these dialogues, the more I conceive of them as experimental processes. And that means that they could be leading towards something unexpected. Behind the scenes, as they say it sometimes happens in chemistry, my interlocutors have already brought me (both methodologically and theoretically) interesting insights that I could not foresee, which I deem fruitful as elements of a possible strategy to renew the museum structure and to make 'participatory' processes stable and sustainable.

One of the best 'good to think with' experiences I have had so far was related to a project that I submitted to the Robert Bosch Foundation and which received financial support to be implemented between 2017 and 2019. The project is titled 'Sharing Heritage: The Cameroon Project, Oku, Stuttgart, Foumban', and its roots lie in the implicit questions posed to me by one of the installations in the past permanent display of the museum's 'Africa' collection. A reconstruction of the entrance to the royal palace and the 'house' of the military society in Elak-Oku, the capital of the kingdom of Oku in northwest Cameroon, was included in the exhibition mounted in the first half of the 1980s. Who were the specific actors behind this installation, and what kind of relationships did they operate within? Northwest Cameroon and Oku in particular were the most prominent research and collecting destinations for Koloss in the 1970s and the 1980s. In Oku, Koloss was granted access in the *kwifon* society, the most powerful political body among the Kingdom's male secret societies, and honoured with the title of *Fai* for cultural affairs, a high-level advisor to the King. I first learnt from a museum's panel that the main elements in the installation were created by Oku's 'best carvers'[13] and then transported to Stuttgart in 1980. Soon, I decided to explore the relationships behind these specific artefacts and the museum and to share my results with the visitors of the new exhibition.

As part of the project, in December 2017 I travelled back to Oku, together with museum director Inés de Castro and Sebastian Sprute, who was doing an internship at the Linden-Museum. What made this apparently traditional networking, research, and documentation project quite special to me was the participation of two other people: Henning Christoph and Stone Karim Mohamad. Christoph is the founder and director of the Soul of Africa Museum in Essen, Germany; after Koloss's death in 2013, Christoph was granted the same honourable title in Oku that Koloss had held. Travelling to Oku with him meant we could count on his local networks for logistical support, and it also offered us a glimpse into the kind of role that Koloss himself might have had in the same context while he was curator at the Linden-Museum. Mohamad, as mentioned above, is a member of the ABRAC, and we were delighted that he agreed to join us in a journey to his country of birth.

During the month we spent together in Cameroon, we joined paths that 'normally' don't cross but rather tend to be parallel and invisible to each other: the museum director making official visits to her counterparts in other countries to

---

13   Koloss had established a stable research and collecting relationship with Fai Mankoh, one of the most highly esteemed masters of carving in Oku, and his apprentices. They carved the poles and door frames for the installation at the Linden-Museum (Koloss 2000, 2015).

explore possible opportunities for international cooperation and exchange; the Africa Department curator exploring a multisited 'field' with a view to giving glimpses of it in an exhibition; the younger colleague exploring life within contemporary European ethnography museums; the private museum director and anthropologist acting as 'gatekeeper'; and finally, a Baden-Württemberg resident who never severed his cultural, political, and spiritual links with the country of his birth and, as poet and photographer, had been researching both contexts himself (and the space of 'in-betweenness') for quite some time.

Each member of the group got a daily-life glimpse into how the others looked at the same contexts and situations, how they acted within them, and what resulted. The major reasons for travelling together were: 1) to explore the past relationship between the Kingdom of Oku and the Linden-Museum and the present relationship between Oku and another German museum, and to possibly establish new ones; and 2) to experiment with a model in which European museums' research in extra-European contexts is developed and conducted in partnership with a member of the 'diaspora' who resides in the city where the museum is located and who is engaged in a 'participatory' process within the same institution. My potentiality (and in some cases wish) to act as a 'bridge' between the two contexts is conceived here, among other things, as a way to help eradicate a notion of human beings as 'pertaining' exclusively to one firmly bounded and defined cultural realm.

Here I focus on one of the unexpected 'outcomes' that I most treasure, which I became aware of right after this dialogue between Mohamad and me took place, as we left Oku for Foumban in December 2017:

'Can I ask you a question?', Mohamad said, 'Not to criticise you, or anything -'
'Sure!', I said, a little worried, as he asked,
'Do you always give your opinion when interviewing people?'

This exchange gave me the chance to explain dialogic anthropology and thus to continue in the healthy exercise of questioning whether what I am doing is grounded in cultural policy and theory, if it is simply a mistake, or both. The moment made me realise one of the unexpected outcomes: Mohamad, attentive like poets can be, could directly and closely witness our methodologies, our views, and our criteria for an object's acquisition. This was a much better platform, I believe, for him to decide whether or not to contribute to projects related to the institution and on what terms. He knows Cameroon very well, and thus knew what he could explore during our journey, what we considered 'our field', and how we constructed it. This put him in a position to better discern if and under what terms to be further involved in future museum activities.

Each individual who joined the ABRAC probably sees the process in a different way, based on their own past and present experience and their visions for the future. This platform gives us the possibility, first of all, to get to know each other; from this process, opportunities come, based on the expertise of each, to also collaborate professionally in order to have an impact on the museum's structure. I hope that we will be able to invest and preserve this precious capital and that in the near future we will be able to start sharing ideas for a new collection strategy. In my view, it is vital that we devotedly contemplate our historical collections, not only because of their sheer significance as historical heritage but also because they are physical testimonies to the colonial *matrix* that lies behind so many contemporary global inequalities, blinding visions, and deafening silences. We might also wish to equip our desired futures with an equally structured vision and collections within which to perform.

We have only taken the first steps in creating a 'community of heritage' around the Linden-Museum's Africa collection, steps that might greatly contribute to the museum's ability to interact with and represent the vibrant multiplexity of today's European cities. The path is not at all easy, tensions not absent, nor is any 'result' predictable or even granted, especially when sustainability is concerned. We are, after all, dancing on thin, burning ice, as Wayne Modest reminded me when discussing this publication. The words of Raymond Silverman (2015, 2) reassured me in this endeavour, in his description of the inherent difficulties in 'collaborative' projects, while also recognising the potential of these institutions as 'spaces in which diverse intellectual, professional and cultural groups can *encounter one another and share activities that lead to new ways of thinking, and to new ways of living*' (emphasis added).

Still, it sounds very good, perhaps too good to be true. It might simply not work. But, if nothing else, attempting 'collaboration is an opportunity to fail in the most splendid way' (Karp quoted in Silverman 2015, 1).

## References

Bouttiaux, A.M., and A. Seiderer, eds. 2011. *Fetish Modernity*. Tervuren: Musée royal de l'Afrique centrale.

Cafuri, R. 2005. *L'arte della migrazione. Memorie africane tra diaspora, arte e musei*. Turin: Trauben.

Clifford, James. 1988. *The Predicament of Culture: Twentieth-Century Ethnography, Literature, and Art*. Cambridge, MA: Harvard University Press.

Ferracuti, S. 2009. 'L'Europa e "gli altr". Cittadinanza e diversità culturale a partire dalle Convenzioni del Consiglio d'Europa'. *Lares* 75, no. 3: 655-70.

Ferracuti, S. 2016. 'Heads and Hands: The Lives and Work of Samson Makamo, Sculptor and Healer in Maputo'. *Tribus* 65: 88-125.

Ferracuti, S., E. Frasca, and V. Lattanzi, eds. 2013. *Beyond Modernity: Do Ethnography Museums Need Ethnography?* Rome: Espera.

Isin, E. 2017. 'Performative Citizenship'. In *The Oxford Handbook of Citizenship*, edited by Ayelet Shachar, Rainer Bauböck, Irene Bloemraad, and Maarten Vink, 500-23. Oxford: Oxford University Press.

Koloss, H-J. 2000. *World-View and Society in Oku Cameroon.* Berlin: Dietrich Reimer Verlag.

Koloss, H-J. 2012. *Cameroon: Thoughts and Memories, Ethnological Research in Oku and Kembong 1975-2005.* Berlin: Dietrich Reimer Verlag.

Marcus, George E. 1997. 'The Uses of Complicity in the Changing Mise-en-Scene of Anthropological Fieldwork'. In *Ethnography through Thick and Thin*, 105-32. Princeton, NJ: Princeton University Press.

Milani, L. 1967. *Lettera a una professoressa.* Florence: LEF.

Mudimbe, V. Y. 1988. *The Invention of Africa.* Bloomington: Indiana University Press.

Munape, K., ed. 2012. [S]*oggetti migranti. Dietro le cose le persone.* Rome: Espera.

Noronha, I., dir. 2007. *Ngwenya, o Crocodilo.* Maputo: Ebano Multimedia.

Padiglione, V. 2002. 'Caaasa!' *Antropologia museale* 1, no. 1: 4-5.

Silverman, Raymond A. 2015. 'Introduction: Museum as Process'. In *Museum as Process: Translating Local and Global Knowledges*, edited by Raymond Silverman, 1-18. New York: Routledge.

Zagato L., and M. Vecco, eds. 2011. *Le culture dell'Europa, l'Europa della cultura.* Milan: Franco Angeli.

Fig. 5.1. Images from podcast series 'Belonging' – Storage area of the Kunstkamera in St Petersburg. Copyright Alana Jelinek.

# Creativity

# Questions of Belonging

ALANA JELINEK

I have been working as an artist for about thirty years. What endures in my practice over the years, irrespective of the medium I use, is an approach that could be called *critically interventionist*. For nine of these years (2009-2018), I was privileged to be invited to intervene directly into the context of ethnographic museums, but I also make interventions that are uninvited and in less defined contexts, such as on public streets, in educational settings, and on the internet.[1] My work in ethnographic museums is focused on questions of 'race' and racism, the legacy of colonialism, and belonging, all questions that inhere in that specific context. My interest in questions of 'race', racism, and the legacy of colonialism also pre-date my work with ethnographic museums. It is, in fact, because of this longer-term interest that I was attracted to working with these museums in the first place. My interest in questions of belonging, though, has emerged since.

Questions of belonging lie just below the surface of any ethnographic collection. Do these things made elsewhere and in other contexts *belong* here in this particular gilded cage, in whichever of the European museums of world cultures? To whom do these things belong – to descendants of the originating culture or descendants of the current host culture? If descendants of those who originally made these things now *belong* here in Europe, as they are here through histories of contact, exchange, and movement forged through centuries of empire, can we say that their material culture also belongs here, even when other descendants who are not here in Europe want it returned to them? How can repatriation be inappropriate and violent in the case of deporting humans who have been deemed 'illegal' by the state, but caring and responsible in the case of things? Given that things, including those that are also ancestors, in ethnographic museums were sometimes collected violently, and always in the context of violence, do they belong here? Or should they be with those who have retained special names, particular knowledge, and exquisite feelings about them, beyond the merely aesthetic? Who belongs and what belongs where are the sub-textual questions playing in the background of any ethnographic museum.

As a person who never felt I belonged in the country to which I was born or within the culture(s) I was raised, questions of belonging felt almost shameful. Inchoate feelings meant these questions were too raw or too deep to address in my work as an artist. (Creating good or great art is not born of unreflective self-expression or unmediated pain, despite Romantic mythologizing to the contrary.) Collaborating with ethnographic museums has enabled me to consciously tackle

---

1   The website www.alanajelinek.com was originally the site for an artwork called 'me-you-them: a diary of racism' in which, for three years from 30 June 2001 to 20 June 2004, I noted every instance of racism that I encountered as a victim, as a bystander and as a perpetrator. It was an intervention into the then-popular online diaries. These have been largely superseded by blogs and vlogs. An archived version remains available on the website www.alanajelinek.com.

questions of belonging and, now liberated from feelings of shame to pursue this question, I realise I had already tackled such questions in my earlier work.

In what follows I explore two such projects: the first a work titled 'Europe the Game', which began in 2003 and has been evolving since. The second is a work entitled 'Belonging', which was made as my final contribution to the multidisciplinary, ambitious research project led by Nicholas Thomas, 'Pacific Presences: Exploring Oceanic Art in European Museums' (funded by the European Research Council, 2013-2018).

## Europe the Game

I was trained originally as a painter, in the days before 'the post-medium condition', when artists were trained in how to be an artist through specific artistic media, such as painting, sculpture, and photography. 'Europe the Game' is a work comprising fifty-four oil paintings. This piece is participatory and performative, where participants in 'the game' are encouraged to interact with and handle the paintings. I started working on this project before I knew whether any gallery would show it. The work emerged in response to the idea of 'Fortress Europe', a critical concept emergent around the turn of the millennium in reaction to the European Union's decision to work on a common immigration policy for Europe, thereby defining the perimeter of Europe and, by implication, the parameters of European-ness. At the time the work was conceived, I would not have imagined that such questioning would have become increasingly relevant, reaching new and more urgent levels in recent years. The questions of who belongs in Europe and what represents 'Europe' remain contested and become ever more urgent with each successive crisis. 'Europe the Game' plays out, and plays with, these questions.

There is a cliché that good art produces questions not answers (in contrast to, according to the cliché, good science). 'Europe the Game' produces neither answers nor questions but playing it embodies the tension inherent in questions of belonging. Engaging with the artwork requires participants to instantiate the tensions within the ideas of belonging, representation, and 'Europe'. Given that the artwork is made of oil paint, questions of value may also arise for some participants but that depends on the sensitivities of its players. (Oil paint is associated to this day with high value and high status and, not unrelatedly, also with the European tradition of painting.) The fifty-four components of 'Europe the Game' are oil-painted bird's-eye views of European 'natural' landscapes. Some are landscapes of stereotypical notions of Europe, including different seasonal views of spring, winter, and summer. Others are landscapes not often associated with Europe. But they are all European. It took me a number of years to paint all fifty-four because most, although not all, are taken from sketches from flights over Europe.

In 'Europe the Game', audiences are invited to choose which of the fifty-four landscapes, painted on wooden panels, fit into a frame that can contain a maximum of thirty-six. The numbers involved are largely arbitrary except that, when playing 'Europe the Game', fifty-four feels like a large but not infinite number, which is an important aspect of how the artwork works. And the emergent Europe produced by the game, which occupies 3.6m² (comprised of thirty-six parts each measuring 60x60cm), is a substantial enough space to make the choices feel significant. The proportion requires that one-third, or eighteen pieces, must be left out.

The rules of the game have been refined over time and there is a video of it being played in Leiden, the Netherlands, in 2016 on YouTube.com, complete with my own preamble and goading comments for the audience/participants (available at: https://www.youtube.com/watch?v=DFyPXwmZQnY). The rules of engagement are summarised below.

### Rules
1) The boundary of Europe is marked
2) Each participant chooses one painting they believe should belong.
3) Each participant places their piece of Europe inside the boundary.
4) Players take turns to fill the marked territory of Europe.
5) When Europe is filled, players negotiate as to which pieces belong in Europe and which must come out.
6) The game ends when all players agree on which belongs.

'Europe the Game' can also be played solo and then it tends to be an exploration of what the player imagines as Europe. Interpretations of the rules seem to change every time it's played. Each context draws out different emphases of location and current preoccupations with the idea of Europe. But the pieces do not change. Nor do the general rules, which are stencilled on the side of the three transport boxes that contain the game:

> 54 factorial permutations of Europe with 54/36 factorial exclusions.

Given that it is an artwork, I will not attempt to convey what 'Europe the Game' does to/for its audiences. Like any artwork, the ideas, knowledge, questions, or impact it carries eschew attempts at translation. Too often artists are required by non-artists to translate their work into other forms of knowledge, to delineate somehow the correct interpretation, to tell audiences what to think, or to describe what audiences think, as if this is possible. And very often, perhaps too often, artists comply. But if an artwork works, it does so in its own terms. It needs no translation.

### Belonging
'Belonging' (2018), by contrast, is a word-based intervention. I have made other word-based artworks, including art-novels, and I also write theory of art about the role and value of art in society. Because I have employed words in both modalities,

in theory and in practice (for want of a better descriptor), I feel I understand the differences between the two and can assert their right to difference. 'Belonging' uses words as its medium, recorded as sound files and edited together in a series of twelve podcasts. I encourage readers of this text to listen for themselves (available at: http://maa.cam.ac.uk/pacific-presences/; https://soundcloud.com/alanajelinek).

It is no accident that 'Belonging' was the final artwork made in the context of a nine-year stint working in ethnographic museums. Not only did the context enable me to address it as it percolated within me, but questions of belonging, for me, lay at the heart of the research project, 'Pacific Presences: Investigating Oceanic Art in European Museums', and 'Belonging' was the culmination of my work at the Museum of Archaeology and Anthropology at the University of Cambridge.

Unlike some institutions that hold historical material culture from elsewhere, such as the National Trust in the United Kingdom, ethnographic museums in Europe seem to consider the ethics behind their collection over and above the question of conservation. Questions of belonging are ever-present. Indigenous groups regularly make demands for the repatriation of artefacts held in national and university collections. Every museum knows that at least some of their collection was gained through nefarious and violent activity. Yet, they also know their collections are the product of genuine and bilateral exchange between chiefs and representatives of the Crown, who were understood locally as chiefs. Sometimes they were exchanges of symbolic, high-status objects on both sides. Some objects in European collections were made specifically for Europeans to take back home and others were collected once they were discarded, especially with the adoption of Christianity. Discarded, once-precious artefacts were often collected by missionaries, either as trophies of souls converted or as usefully alarming material to inspire greater fundraising back home. Missionary collections often subsequently found their way into museums. I did not understand this complexity when I first began working with the Museum of Archaeology and Anthropology in 2009. The stereotype of ethnographic museums I entertained was as trophy cabinets of empire. My thinking on this was informed by exhibitions such as *Trophies of Empire* in 1993, organised by artist Keith Piper, with Bluecoat Gallery, Arnolfini Gallery, Hull Time Based Arts, and Liverpool John Moores University, which occurred at a similar time to the internationally renowned intervention by Fred Wilson, 'Mining the Museum', at the Maryland Historical Society, in Baltimore, MD, in the United States.

Their concurrence (with no doubt many further examples) demonstrates a paradigm shift in museum practice in the early 1990s. With the scholarly change in approaches to museums in the mid-1980s, collectively known as the 'New Museology', artists began to be invited to engage with historical museum collections in order to draw out their nascent plurivocality, the hitherto unacknowledged coexistence of multiple, divergent, and conflicting voices, including the previously absent 'subaltern' voice, to use the expression made current by postcolonial theorist Gayatri

Spivak (1993). Until this point, museums had largely celebrated empire, colonial rule, and either white supremacist beliefs or unexamined assumptions about European ascendancy. Or they promulgated the benefits of subjugation and exploitation for both the dominant and the dominated.

Since inviting in the voice of the Other through artistic and 'source community' interventions has become the new norm in reflexive museum practice, it is perhaps the perfect time to turn our attention to the complexity of the notion of nation (or 'race', ethnicity, culture, or any other monolithic term) and the people that comprise it. Many artists and scholars already bring to consciousness the multicultural complexity and intercultural crossings that render it impossible to label any single individual in relation to any single culture, language, 'race', nation, or place of 'origin', as Édouard Glissant ([1990] 1997) describes it. The artwork 'Belonging' aims also to bring to consciousness such complexity.

For 'Belonging', the question of whether we can think about things in the diaspora the same way that we think about people living in the diaspora was uppermost in my mind. I knew that some artefacts are ancestors, sometimes literally so, and seeing them as human ancestors stirred me to wonder: if they are indeed human, how can anyone say they don't belong here? To explore this, I interviewed a range of ethnography curators from Europe and the Pacific, some of whom have mixed and indigenous heritage and most of whom have only European heritage. I also interviewed various people who identify as indigenous from a range of places and backgrounds living in the diaspora. Added to this was the serendipitous recording of Australian Aboriginal repatriation activist of Gweagal descent, Rodney Kelly, during his visit to the Museum of Archaeology and Anthropology in 2016 in order to open up dialogue about repatriating the spears and other things taken from his ancestors when they encountered Captain Cook in 1770.

Questions for the curators included: How do you feel about the repatriation of things back to the place where they were made? How do you prevent your own culture from getting in the way of how you understand or engage with the objects from other cultures in your museum? And, what is your own cultural background? Questions for indigenous people included: What is your cultural background (or *whakapapa*, a Maori concept of lineage) and where do you live now? How do you feel about objects from your culture being in museums in Europe? And, how do you feel about questions of belonging? Because each participant knew the project was called 'Belonging', many chose to respond to this concept even when they weren't directly asked about it.

The art-podcasts were compiled using recordings of interviews with Julie Adams, Lilja Kapua Addeman, Susanna Rianna Balai, Liz Bonshek, Insos Ireeuw, Rodney Kelly, Emelihter Kihleng, Oliver Lueb, Kolokesa Māhina-Tuai, Ole Maiava, Sean Mallon, Imelda Miller, Wayne Modest, Pala Molisa, Rick Pa, Pandora Fulimalo Pereira, Jackie Shown, Maria Stanyukovich, Reina Sutton, Kat Szabo, Nina Tonga, Alisa Vavataga, Fanny Wonu Veys, Kaetaeta Watson, and Maria Wronska Friend.

Snippets of the interviews, which were ten to twenty minutes in length, were edited into smaller bites of fifteen, thirty, or sixty seconds. Each of the final art-podcasts is nine to ten minutes in length; throughout, the short snippets are juxtaposed, sometimes overlapping, and sometimes repeated. I tried to anticipate what would be sympathetic to hear and what would be challenging or annoying, and I tried to maintain a balance of sympathies both within one podcast and across the complete series. At all times I was mindful of respecting the perspective of the contributor, and I never edited anyone against the grain of what I understood they had wanted to say. Each contributor was sent a link to the recording in order to choose to delete any part they might want not to share. None took up this option.

I launched the series with a podcast that encapsulated all the issues at stake in these questions, setting the scene for the subsequent podcasts. The final podcast is the least linear, the least narrative in structure, and the podcasts in between offer a range of different inputs, perspectives, and editing experiments. My aim was to try to ensure sympathy for each of the speakers at some point over the series. If a person offers challenging or orthodox views at one point, this was softened by an additional snippet or counterpoint at some other point. What I hope is that a listener feels the complexity within the questions of belonging and a sympathy for this complexity. Online, each of the podcasts is supplemented by a little contextual information and a photo taken either by me or by Mark Adams, whose art practice treads similar ground to my own.

'Belonging' is an 'emotive word', to quote Liz Bonshek, then of Melbourne Museum in her interview for the podcasts. She makes this observation as a criticism of the 'Belonging' project because, she argues, no one speaks about belonging. She, a dual-national, doesn't think about belonging unless someone asks, and none of the indigenous people she knows or works with talk about belonging. But I know otherwise. A sense of belonging is one of those privileges that goes overlooked if a person has it. Those without it long for it. It is one of the many losses resultant from colonialism; it is another of the losses that have not been addressed and are perceived either as not a problem or as the invention of postcolonial obsessives. On some level this might be true. Once we, all of us, including those who feel they belong and those who feel they don't, decolonise our minds, questions of belonging may be settled.

## References

Glissant, Édouard. 1997. *Poetics of Relation*. Translated from French by Betsy Wing. Originally published in 1990. Ann Arbor: University of Michigan Press.

Spivak, Gayatri Chakravorty. 1993. 'Can the Subaltern Speak?' In *Colonial Discourse and Post-Colonial Theory: A Reader*, edited by Patrick Williams and Laura Chrisman, 70-75. Hemel Hempstead: Harvester Wheatsheaf.

Fig. 5.2. Image of podcast series, 'Belonging', MAA, Cambridge. Copyright Alana Jelinek.

Fig. 5.3. 'The Fork's Tale' at the Museum of Archaeology and Anthropology, Cambridge. Copyright Alana Jelinek.

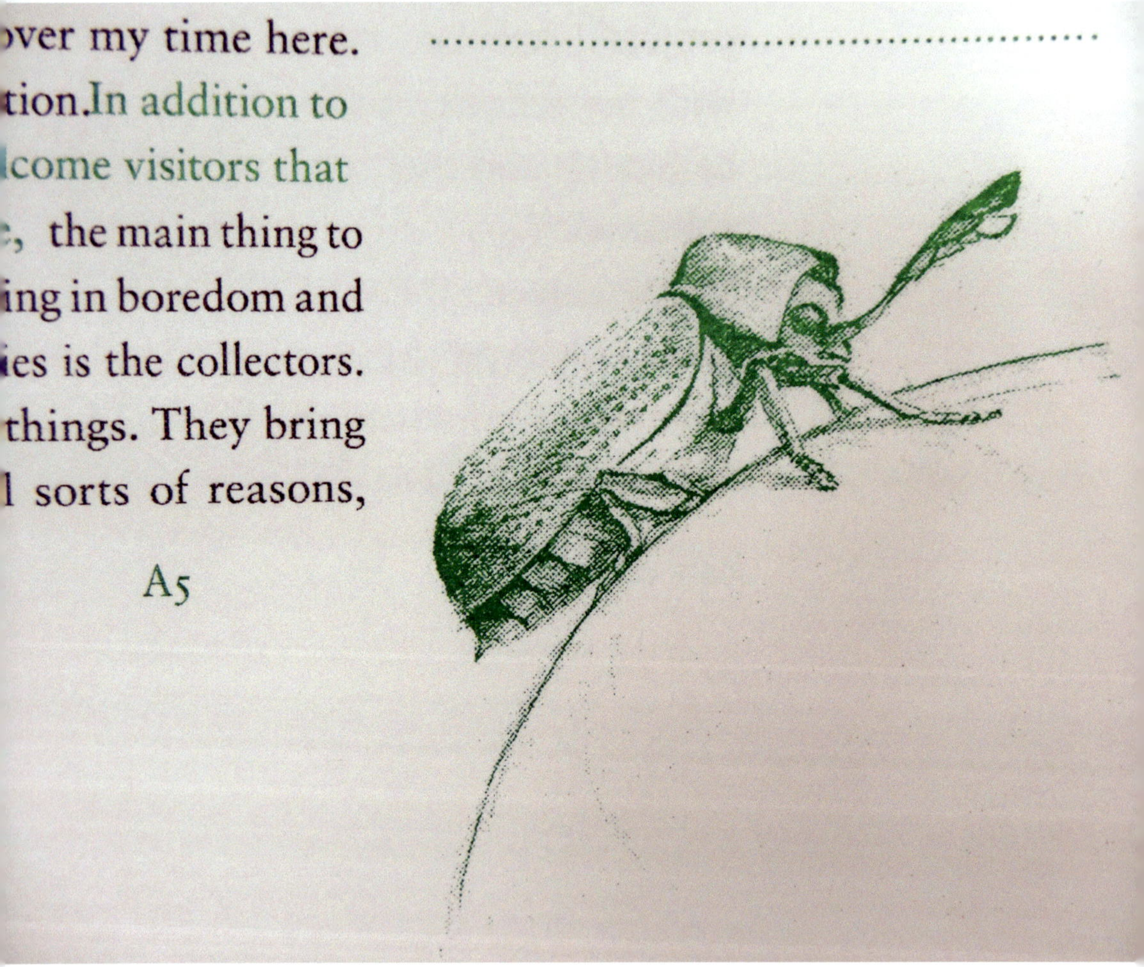

over my time here.
tion. In addition to
come visitors that
, the main thing to
ing in boredom and
ies is the collectors.
things. They bring
l sorts of reasons,

A5

Fig. 5.4. Detail from 'The Fork's Tale', as Narrated by Itself.
Copyright Alana Jelinek.

Fig. 5.5. First page of 'The Fork's Tale', as Narrated by Itself. Copyright Alana Jelinek.

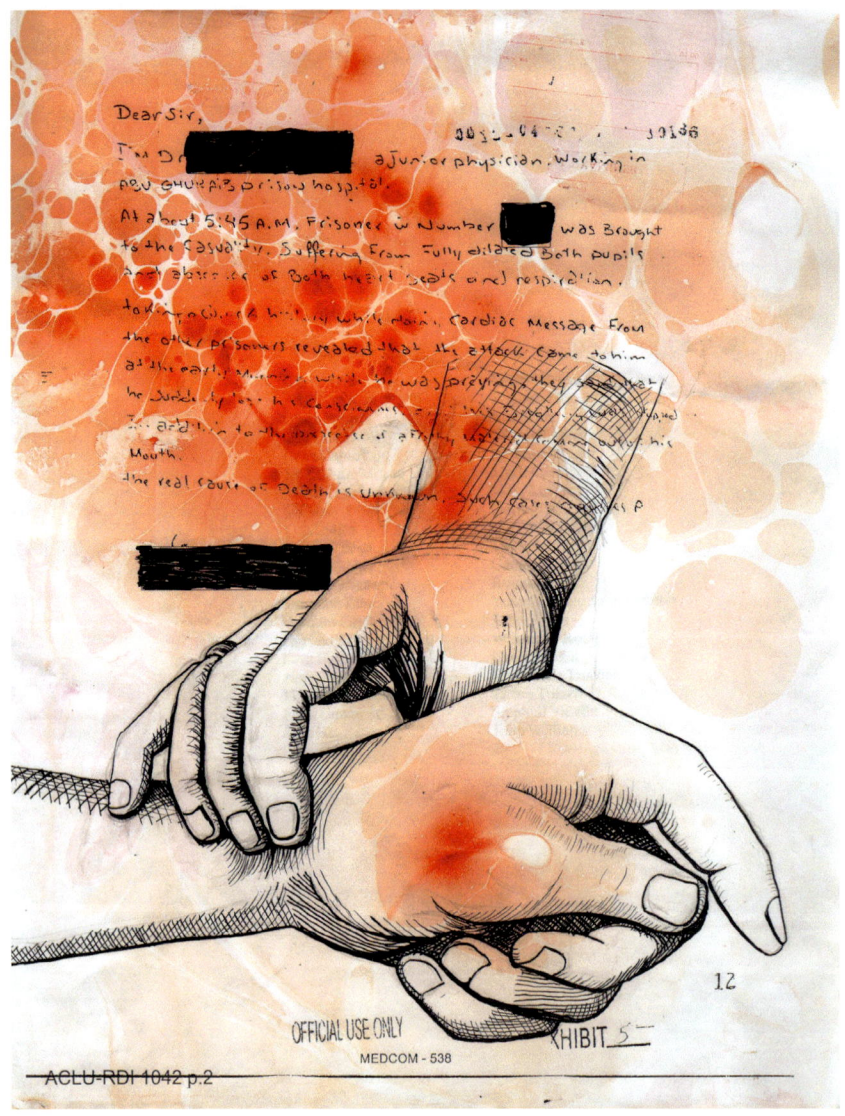

Fig. 6.1. From 'Did You Kiss the Dead Body?', marbled US military autopsy report and ink, Rajkamal Kahlon 2012. Copyright Rajkamal Kahlon.

# Love and Loss in the Ethnographic Museum

RAJKAMAL KAHLON

## 1.

Empathy is understood as the ability to feel or enter into the emotions of another. The science fiction writer Octavia Butler, in her dystopic novels *Parable of the Sower* (1993) and *Parable of the Talents* (1998), created a main character who suffers from an affliction called 'hyper-empathy syndrome', which is characterised by the inability to observe someone in pain without likewise feeling pain to debilitating effect. This character directly experiences the pain and pleasure of others and is frequently incapacitated by the violence unfolding around her. With this ability, or affliction, she gains insight into others through a process that threatens the limits of herself.

DATE OF BIRTH:
DATE OF DEATH: 3 December 2002
DATE OF AUTOPSY: 6-8 December 2002
INVESTIGATIVE AGENCY: USACIDC, SSI # 0134-02-CID369-23533-5H9B

I. CIRCUMSTANCES OF DEATH: The decedent is a 27-28 year old Pashtun male, who was found unresponsive, restrained in his cell, Bagram Collection Point (BCP), 0015, 4 December 2002. He was dead on arrival at the 339th CSH, Bagram Air Field, Afganistan.

II. AUTHORIZATION: Armed Forces Medical Examiner under Title 10 U.S. Code, Section 1471.

III. IDENTIFICATION: Visual recognition:

Fig. 6.2. From the project, 'Did You Kiss the Dead Body?' This material was excerpted from US Department of Defense Document 003146, one of many obtained by the ACLU through the Freedom of Information Act. These documents described Iraqi and Afghan men being killed in American military prisons and their bodies subjected to autopsies.

I sit in the audience at the Reckoning with History conference and start having what could be called a hysterical physical response. I've experienced this before in ethnographic museums. The last time this happened I was at the Weltmuseum Wien, for the opening of my exhibition, *Staying with Trouble*.

My right eye begins reacting to the conference presentations with violent impatience, twitching uncontrollably. I try to will it into submission. The result is failure. My body rebels even as I try to perform the role of the good audience member, erect and frozen posture, silent, notebook in hand. I am waiting to recognise the concepts being thrown around, one dispassionate gesture after another. I hear 'colonialism', 'ethnography', and 'museums', repeated again and again into the microphone. Where theft and the most barbaric orders of violence once dwelled, there are only empty linguistic markers left, devoid of any recognisable meaning. Are we talking about the same thing? I feel a scream building in my belly which I quickly suppress and transform into a familiar taste of acidity and bitterness.

VIII. OPINION: Based on these autopsy findings and the investigative and historical information available to me, the cause of death of this Pashtun male, [b)(6)-4] is pulmonary embolism (blood clot that traveled to the heart and blocked the flow of blood to the lungs). The patterned abrasion on the back of the left calf is consistent with the tread of a boot. The severe injury to the underlying calf muscle and soft tissue is most likely a contributing factor. The deceased was not under the pharmacologic effects of drugs or alcohol at the time of death. Therefore, the manner of death, in my opinion is homicide.

LTC (P), MC, USA
Armed Forces Regional Medical Examiner

Fig. 6.3. From the project, 'Did You Kiss the Dead Body?'

As an artist, I delve into histories we'd rather not remember, histories of brutal violence that lay beneath our feet but are skilfully ignored. I immerse myself in these histories only to frequently experience nausea, grief, and rage. I have physical symptoms as well. Shortness of breath, clenched stomach, tightness in my chest and lungs, dizziness, rapid heart rate – all the physiological indicators of a fear-induced, fight-or-flight response. It is our survival that is at stake in these archives, these museum collections, and these representations of our histories. To experience history as an embodied subject in a way that can invade your deepest interior spaces means transcending representation and moving into the realm of somatic experience.

**B. EXTERNAL EXAMINATION:** The remains are those of a well developed, well nourished Southwest Asian male of muscular build that appears compatible with the listed age of 27-28 years. Length is 5 feet, 4 inches. The body is well preserved and has not been embalmed. Multiple injuries are described below in the Evidence of Injury Section.

Fig. 6.4. From the project, 'Did You Kiss the Dead Body?'

Colonialism is now. It never died. It is stronger than ever. Facilitated by new technologies, the evidence of its destruction is growing. Europe's borders won't hold. The ethnographic museum's only hope is to understand that it is a holocaust museum. Once this conceptual shift can be made, we can deal with the real work at hand – making something that can heal out of this vast landscape of trauma.

For me this has meant being in contact with the source of the trauma. I look at the visual records of colonialism, carefully searching for moments that can reveal something about the world I've inherited and now must inhabit. Contact and acceptance, as opposed to denial, are only the beginning of the process. Next, I try to understand what the images are saying to me. They can speak if I listen closely. Their speech is one layer. They provoke deep emotional responses in me which also need decoding. Then the intangibles of time and reflection are added into the brew. Patience is required. And attention. It can be instantaneous, or it might take a few days, weeks, or years to have a coherent understanding of what my course of action might be in relation to the traumatic material before me.

A recent project called 'Do You Know Our Names?' is one such response to the central role of ethnographic photography within larger colonial projects. In one way you could say that my twenty years of study and contact with the visual legacies of colonialism all come to bear in this project. There is a visual arch operating in the work that moves between calling attention to the violence of the original image and moving past it into a gesture of healing and redemption. Photographic reproductions found in the German anthropology book *Die Völker der Erde* are enlarged in new reproductions which I then paint over. In part, I am retracing the steps of nineteenth-century photographers who hand-coloured their photographs. But where the goal for them was a heightened fidelity to the photograph, mine is to radically alter it. I am attempting a rehabilitation of the humanity, individuality, and beauty of the women originally depicted. Transformed with contemporary clothing, fashionable hairstyles, and makeup, the women make a shift from anonymous anthropological subjects into modern individuals who command the viewer's attention.

As an artist I have found, after many years of trial and error, a way of entering into empathic relationships with traumatic histories and creating, at least for myself, new possibilities of healing. Perhaps Octavia Butler's hyper-empathic heroine can also be a model for transforming traumatic experience into positive structural change, in place of the seemingly endless replications of violence we now live with.

## 2. You Said It Wouldn't Hurt: Love and Loss at the Weltmuseum Wien

I have a love-hate relationship to ethnographic museums. They literally make me ill, yet like a car accident or a train wreck, I can't look away. In 2016, full of doubts, I went to work for two months as the SWICH artist-in-residence at the Weltmuseum Wien, formerly Das Museum für Völkerkunde. Would I be a 'native' informant? A shamanic priest exorcising the burden of guilt carried by the ethnographic museum? Would I be a neoliberal artistic cheerleader adding value to their brand? Probably all of these questions could be answered in the affirmative, yet I still wanted to go. I wanted to make an intimate examination of my patient, to glimpse beneath the hemline at the beauty and horror of protruding objects and spiritual deformations. Before going, my strategy was to get as close as I could, kick very hard, and then run like hell. Cowardly? Perhaps. If my residency had been a film, the script might call for my character to have a reoccurring nightmare of waking up each morning as a new object in the museum's collections, tagged, photographed, and inventoried.

I came to the Weltmuseum Wien as an anthropologist might to view the natives up close. I photographed everyone I met and created a travel diary titled *Field Work: An Artist's Reflection among Her Time with the Natives of Vienna, illustrated with numerous watercolors and handwritten, 2016,* modelled after popular nineteenth-century colonial travel diaries. At the museum I encountered a staff that had their own ambivalence and complicated relationship to its violent history, while simultaneously performing care for the objects contained in its collections. Among the staff there were many skilled and unskilled workers who had short-term and temporary contracts. Almost all were women. The men, in contrast, held positions of power in the museum, collecting comparatively generous salaries and garnering greater social prestige. The staff was also almost exclusively white. The museum may have a new name, but colonial habits die hard. Vast structural inequalities tied to race, gender, and class remain unchanged.

Going in, I had many judgements of ethnographic museums. Chief among them was that they are steeped in a foundational and existential form of colonial violence and thus are very likely unredeemable. In the contemporary ethnographic museum, there's a scramble for politically correct language and a desperate need to be on the right side of history. This very desire to be right is rooted in a binary philosophical understanding of the world, one that doesn't allow the museum to understand its complex entanglements in the perpetuation and reproduction of new forms of colonial violence. For me, walking into an ethnographic museum is like walking into a holocaust museum, but one that doesn't understand its history or its purpose. Ethnographic museums unknowingly aided in the destruction of the majority of the world's cultures and they now celebrate the material evidence of that destruction. And in nearly the same breath, they aim to become pro-migrant, multicultural community spaces supporting the very communities they once helped to defame. Today, schizophrenic gestures abound in the ethnographic museum.

And yet, after everything is said and done, I was seduced. I didn't understand it at the time but now, two years later, I realise that the exhibition I made for the museum, *Staying with Trouble*, was an act of love, a kind of love letter to the Weltmuseum Wien. I hope the museum will one day embrace its message. At the end of my residency, I could have just left a few traces and half-musings about what it meant to be there. This was all that was expected after the two-month residency. But the people I found trapped inside the Weltmuseum Wien's photo archive kept calling me closer, asking me to speak with them, asking for a way out. The need to care for, rehabilitate, and transform the traces of these people and the cultures that have for so long been distorted, maligned, and erased by institutions like the Weltmuseum Wien was too powerful to refuse. I couldn't turn away. During the next eighteen months, with my contract to the museum already fulfilled, I crafted a love letter to the men and women who are still in that archive, and ultimately to the museum itself. *Staying with Trouble* is the closest I've come as an artist to wearing my heart on my sleeve.

## References

Butler, Octavia. 1993. *Parable of the Sower*. New York: Four Walls Eight Windows.
Butler, Octavia. 1998. *Parable of the Talents*. New York: Seven Stories Press.

Fig. 6.5. 'Untitled', from the series 'Do You Know Our Names?', ink, gouache and acrylic on archival digital print, Rajkamal Kahlon, 2017. Photo: Uta Neumann, copyright Rajkamal Kahlon.

Fig. 6.6. 'Woman with Skull', gouache and ink on watercolor paper, Rajkamal Kahlon, 2017. Copyright Rajkamal Kahlon.

Fig. 6.7. Detail from installation 'Die Völker der Erde' [People of the Earth], ink, gouache and acrylic on bookpage, Rajkamal Kahlon, 2017. Copyright Rajkamal Kahlon.

Fig. 6.8. Installation photo, Rajkamal Kahlon: 'Staying With Trouble', Weltmuseum Wien, 2017, photographer: Michael Michlmayr. Copyright Rajkamal Kahlon.

Fig. 7.1. Installation view 'Eyes in the Back of Your Head', Kunstverein Harburger Bahnhof, Hamburg, 2017. Courtesy of Bianca Baldi and Kunstverein Harburger Bahnhof. Photo: Michael Pfisterer.

# Eyes in the Back of Your Head: A Talisman Against Disillusionment

BIANCA BALDI

Knowledge is never without desire; there is a drive to know, a desire to understand, to make sense of, and maybe even own. Knowledge is always unattainable and impossible to incorporate or consume entirely, so it is this urge that keeps fuelling the drive from fragment to fragment in hope of attaining the whole object of desire. *Sapere aude.*

When offered an open invitation to probe and exhume, to examine teeth and bones, the relics and trophies of journeys past, one is always filled with suspicion. There is a sense that there is something at stake. While collections hold tangible artefacts, what piques my interest is not visible or tangible but rather the invisible infrastructures or technologies upon which many ethnographic collections are built, fuelled by the desire for knowledge.

You could say that knowledge hinges on a shared belief. Disillusionment, on the other hand, is that feeling of disappointment when you discover that something is not as good as you believed it to be.

## The Invisible Empire

I received such an open invitation from the Slovene ethnographic museum in Ljubljana. This was not the first project in which I worked with colonial artefacts housed in ethnographic collections. In fact, my first involvement with such a collection did not encounter such open doors. Instead, I was faced with many red flags and barriers long before gaining access to the objects. It was precisely this experience that led me to consider the ever-present invisible infrastructures of power that became the subject of my project 'Eyes in the Back of Your Head'. The project took up the historical shift in how we think about power, moving from a centralised point to invisible transmissions to an invisible empire.

'Eyes in the Back of Your Head' was inspired by a collection of black and white images housed by the Slovene ethnographic museum. The images were taken by Slovene engineer Anton Codelli during the construction of Funkstation Kamina, a radio tower in construction from 1911 to 1914 near the village Kamina in Togo. Codelli had been commissioned by the German telecommunications company Telefunken, which erected the tower in its former colony with the bold aim to be the first to connect Europe (Brandenburg) and Africa (Kamina) wirelessly. It was precisely this aim which prompted me to consider the nature of twentieth-century imperial power, and how it hinged on a modern-era belief in progress and technology. The hand of power could now reach remotely, creating invisible networks between the German colonies in Swakopmund and Dar es Salaam and back to Germany. The network as contemporary sublime.

As a counterpoint, a second artefact drew my attention: a two-dimensional talisman found inside the engineer's briefcase. This remarkable object worked much like the tower by using an infrastructure, only this time a magical infrastructure of text and illustration. Most talismans rely on a symbolic value: think of a nazar, an eye-shaped amulet, for example, which functions on the symbolic level to ward off the 'evil eye'. The engineer's talisman, on the other hand, suggests an architectural space that is inscribed by the cleric. Colloquially this construction is referred to as the fort (نصح), the stronghold, the tower. The evil is not warded off through symbolic means but rather is coaxed into the magical infrastructure that the talisman creates, its invisible empire.

## The Documents are Sufficient Proof for the Introduction of the Problem of Reality

Such a talisman is created in direct consultation with a cleric. Your ill is explained and in response to this, a bespoke fortress is constructed to capture your woe. But this structure is not meant to stand forever; the talisman is portable and disposable. Although it is held close to your heart, once the magic has worked, there is no longer a need to hold on to the document as proof.

The ruins of Funkstation Kamina still persist in the landscape of Togo today. It took over three years to build the station, and the structure was never intended to be temporary. But when World War I started, the Germans destroyed it themselves so it wouldn't fall into the hands of Britain or France. Only a couple of messages were exchanged via the towering steel structures, traveling a distance of over 5000km.

> *Eurer Hoheit entbietet aus der deutschen Heimat auf drahtlosem Wege über 5000 km ihre untertänigst. Grüsse die Telefunkenstation Nauen.*
>
> *Eure Hoheit is Adolf Friedrich zu Mecklenburg, the last Gouverneur of German Colony Togo.*

Colonial collections persist and hold on to their material proof but still confront their ghosts alone. The infrastructures that were constructed still influence the way we live today. 'Eyes in the Back of Your Head' is a talisman against disillusionment. It is a means to dispel the well-learned illusion that Western imperialism still upholds: that is the pursuit of knowledge to conceive a narrative of progress and innovation which forgives the violence of imperialism, the problem of reality.

## I Come to You Because I Desire to See

If you have eyes in the back of your head, you are bestowed a second sight that transcends the physical limitations of your eyes. From this uncanny perspective you survey all aspects simultaneously. The anthropologist Ernesto de Martino's work on magic, in his 1959 book *Sud e Magia*[1], reminds us that there are various forms of reality and that belief is central to producing any system of knowledge. For de Martino it's not important whether it's rational or not; the central question is why the anti-magic argument, which runs through the veins of Western thinking, became a problem of or question about knowledge. Knowledge is not the singular truth upon which museum collections are built. Seeing is not necessarily believing.

'Eyes in the Back of Your Head' points to magic and telecommunication's shared vocabulary: the medium, the transmission, the message. And while so much vocabulary is common, a shared belief is still challenging to find. From mysticism to the scientific method, it is all based on belief, only historically 'the West' was inclined to believe its version of reality, and anything outside of this universal perspective has been dismissed as superstition. Always hovering above what is accepted as truth. Working in colonial collections today, we are forced to see these illusions and to reckon with modernity's inability to see the ghosts. I come to you because I desire to see.

---

1   De Martino, E. 1959 (2001). *Sud e magia*. Feltrinelli Editore.

Fig. 7.2. Installation view 'Eyes in the Back of Your Head', Kunstverein Harburger Bahnhof, Hamburg, 2017. Courtesy of Bianca Baldi and Kunstverein Harburger Bahnhof. Photo: Michael Pfisterer.

Fig. 7.3. Detail. Eyes in The Back of Your Head (2017). Video and steel construction, acrylic one-way mirror, monitor 142 X 82 X 82 cm
Copyright: Courtesy Bianca Baldi and Kunstverein Harburger Bahnhof. Photo: Michael Pfisterer.

Fig. 7.4. a-e. Video Stills. Eyes in The Back of Your Head (2017). Video and steel construction, acrylic one-way mirror, monitor. 142 X 82 X 82 cm
Video credits: 08:23 min (looped), colour, stereo
Animation: GVN 908 Sound: Christophe Albertijn Voice: Jana Haeckel.
Copyright: Courtesy Bianca Baldi.

Fig. 7.4. a-e. Video Stills. Eyes in The Back of Your Head (2017). Video and steel construction, acrylic one-way mirror, monitor. 142 X 82 X 82 cm
Video credits: 08:23 min (looped), colour, stereo
Animation: GVN 908 Sound: Christophe Albertijn Voice: Jana Haeckel.
Copyright: Courtesy Bianca Baldi.

Fig. 7.4. a-e. Video Stills. Eyes in The Back of Your Head (2017). Video and steel construction, acrylic one-way mirror, monitor. 142 X 82 X 82 cm
Video credits: 08:23 min (looped), colour, stereo
Animation: GVN 908 Sound: Christophe Albertijn Voice: Jana Haeckel.
Copyright: Courtesy Bianca Baldi.

Fig. 7.4. a-e. Video Stills. Eyes in The Back of Your Head (2017). Video and steel construction, acrylic one-way mirror, monitor. 142 X 82 X 82 cm
Video credits: 08:23 min (looped), colour, stereo
Animation: GVN 908 Sound: Christophe Albertijn Voice: Jana Haeckel.
Copyright: Courtesy Bianca Baldi.

Fig. 7.4. a-e. Video Stills. Eyes in The Back of Your Head (2017). Video and steel construction, acrylic one-way mirror, monitor. 142 X 82 X 82 cm
Video credits: 08:23 min (looped), colour, stereo
Animation: GVN 908 Sound: Christophe Albertijn Voice: Jana Haeckel.
Copyright: Courtesy Bianca Baldi.

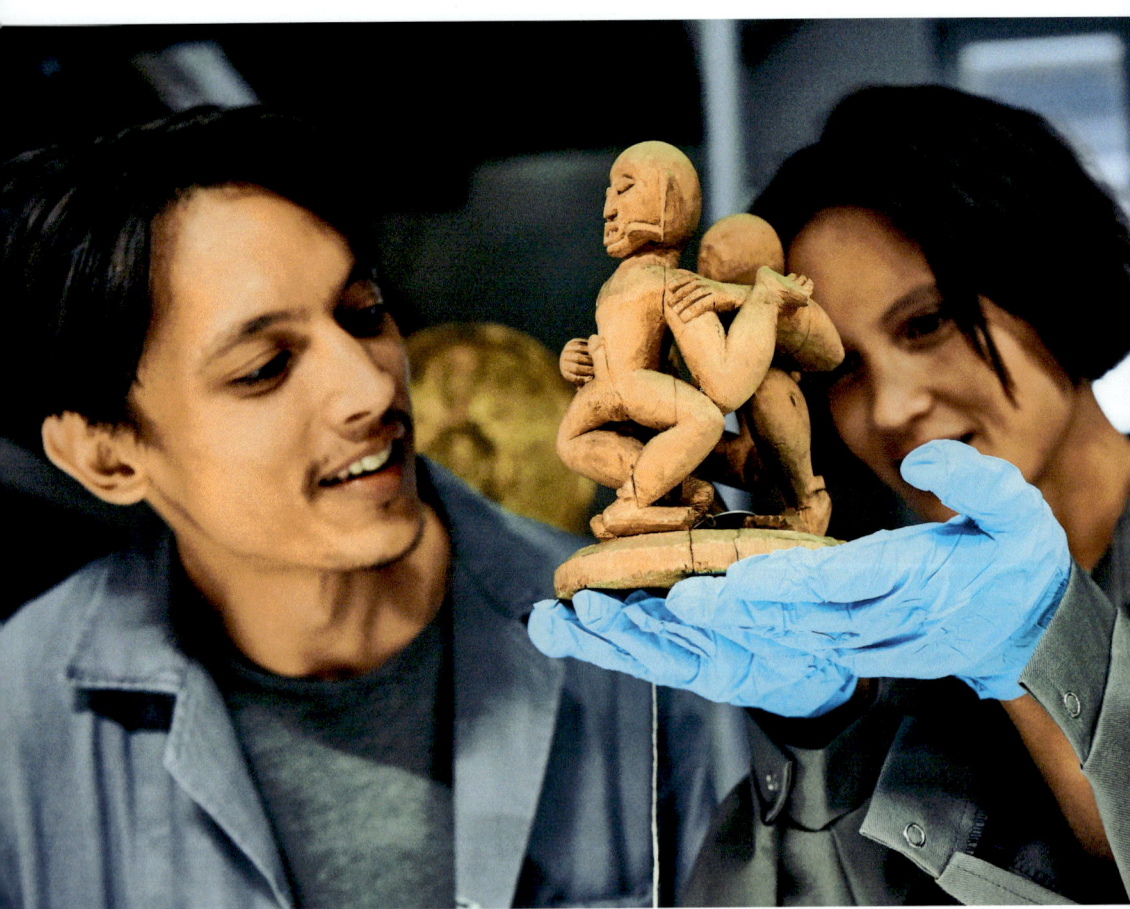

Fig. 8.1. *Antonina Boschitsch and Florian Boschitsch.* Photo by Aleksandra Pawloff for the exhibition *Out of the Box* at Weltmuseum Wien, Vienna.

# I Came as a Stranger

ALEKSANDRA PAWLOFF

1.

As a photographer, my subject is people. In my work, I am interested in the person beyond their appearance. I want to elicit from the viewer a feeling of connection with my subjects, to touch the viewer, not to please or shock them. Simultaneously, I work to reveal the unknown or unacknowledged, even darker, sides of my subject, sides that have been successfully suppressed in daily life. With the greatest of respect, I want to trigger the viewer's emotional engagement with the person pictured, wherever that person lives. In my experience, human beings are never fundamentally different from one another, whether I encounter them in a village in Niger or a park in Vienna.

Yet the 'otherness' of my subjects – their apparent or presumed difference – is often what informs much of the discourse around the present and future of Europe today, and it is what many people seem to fear. I have often wondered whether that feeling of not belonging or being regarded as an outsider is any less threatening than the feeling of having 'too many others' entering one's 'own' territory. Today, this fear of otherness emanates from right-wing governments and movements all over Europe. The mental mechanism of exclusion has always been the first step towards the mass murder of 'others' in a world that is quickly becoming smaller. But what might have been a survival strategy that worked in the Stone Age, when we roamed large spaces in small groups, is no longer valid in the multicultural world we live in today.

What could be a more appropriate place for thinking about us and others than the museum, which has long functioned as a repository for things unknown, a place for the 'adoration of the exotic'? Just think of all the people coming to admire the Penacho in the Weltmuseum Wien. What better place to reconcile us with the presumed otherness of others? Such a task of reconciliation is not straightforward, nor can it be achieved by merely exhibiting things that have until only recently been catalogued according to Western scientific categories. Indeed, such practices have long been criticised as an expression of the symbolic power over and subjugation of the other, enacted through belittling eyes. We could even suggest that this outmoded gaze corresponds precisely to the way we look upon strangers today, upon places and nations represented by the museum in uncritical and unreflective ways.

2.

I vividly remember walking into Block 17, the Austrian memorial place in the Auschwitz concentration camp, in 1999 and being faced with the words: *Austria was the first victim of National Socialism*. It has taken until 2009 for the Austrian government to reconsider this view of ourselves as victims and to acknowledge the undeniable enthusiasm with which many Austrians collaborated with the Nazis. In that year, Block 17 was redesigned as a memorial, acknowledging Austria's complicity in Nazism. In 2013 this display was closed and a new concept is still being developed. Such approaches to history have been changing in the last two decades and Austria, always slower it seems, follows this trend.

The Weltmuseum Wien, Austria's largest ethnographic museum, reopened last year with a radically new approach. It moved away from being a heritage museum focussed on the past towards a people-centred place, aware and willing to take up the responsibility that comes with recognising that a 'museum is a political space that can influence the way people conceive and understand one another and the world they live in' (Onciul 2013, 81). It was with this commitment that the museum organised the collaborative exhibition *Out of the Box – Moving Worlds*.

In this exhibition, the museum invited thirty people of different backgrounds, all based in Vienna, to choose objects from the museum's collections to which they felt some connection. The group was comprised of academics and artists, in general open-minded and well-educated individuals, and many were friends or close acquaintances of the guest curator who selected the participants. Compared to a similar project, *Creatures of Earth and Sky*, described by Serena Iervolino (2013) as an intercultural dialogue project with African migrants living in Parma, Italy, the people involved in *Out of the Box* represented an intellectual and cultural elite.

As both a participant in and photographer of the project, it was my task to document the emotions, whether curiosity, surprise, or enthusiasm, of each person as they came into contact with the object that they had chosen. Feelings arose and thoughts were triggered about what 'home' and 'origin' mean. Did the encounter with the object elicit a longing for home or questions about origins? Did participants think about where they are from and how they define themselves in relation to their chosen object? Why did they choose that particular object and not another? The objects stopped being mere objects and gained significance for each of us, while at the same time we gave the objects meanings they did not previously have. The outcome – written texts and the video-recorded interviews – was a highly professional and thoughtful reflection on origins, home, and roots/routes in connection with the chosen objects.

3.
For me, as a politically engaged photographer, a question that frequently arises in my work is: how can I reach out to and involve a large variety of people in what I do, including people who may be afraid of the otherness of the so-called stranger? I am especially interested in reaching those who, due to their fear, 'are not willing to look at each other as human beings', as Timothy Zaal, a self-proclaimed white supremacist-turned-pacifist, says in the Museum of Tolerance, where he talks to visitors every week (Golding 2013).

One year ago I started a project that I named 'Fremd bin ich gekommen' (I Came as a Stranger), a slight alteration of the first line of the poem *Good Night* from *Die Winterreise* written by Wilhelm Müller (1823). This work was forbidden under Metternich's authoritarian regime (1809-1948) and was set to music by Franz Schubert, who stood in opposition to that regime. I have been photographing and interviewing people with a migrant background, defined in Austria as having a father or a mother born outside Austria. They make up one-half of the Viennese population. I have spoken with grocers, construction and health care workers, musicians, teachers, cleaning personnel, managers, pizza delivery workers, students, professors, the old and the young, men and women. I have walked into restaurants, bookshops, barbershops, tramways, bakeries, and clothing stores. I have written to schools, homes for the elderly, and hospitals, and have asked people to work with me. I have portrayed people of a specific district and exhibited that work in their district. Then I move on to another district. I have focussed on local neighbourhoods because they constitute familiar environments where people can recognise each other and feel safe.

Vienna, like every city in the world, was created thanks to people coming from other places and has always been a lively combination of people of different nationalities. By showing portraits alongside personal biographies, and doing so in neighbourhoods and among neighbours, I hope to make viewers see that there is no need to fear newcomers. Very soon they too will be part of Vienna, just like the people in my portraits who speak about what home means to them, how they relate to Vienna versus their country of origin, how they were treated by the Viennese as children, what they love and what they fear. Each story is unique, emotional, surprising, and thoughtful. I do believe that 'the very personal is what changes people's consciousness', as Shirley Gunn, a South African activist and director of the Human Rights Media Centre in Cape Town, argued in a 2011 interview with the International Coalition of Sites of Conscience[1].

The places I choose to show these works have a very low threshold of exclusion; they are where people go in the course of their everyday lives, such as adult education centres or public administration buildings. The hospital is an ideal place. I cannot think of a place where people come more randomly, have more time available, and are at the same time vulnerable, closer to 'the crack in everything' that is 'how the light gets in' (Leonard Cohen, 'Anthem').

---

1 '"The Very Personal Is What Changes People's Consciousness": An Interview with Activist Shirley Gunn', *International Coalition of Sites of Conscience*, accessed 1 June 2018. https://www.sitesofconscience.org/en/shirley-gunn/.

4.

In contrast to those in the museum, the objects in my exhibitions are not things but people and their lives. I am convinced that people who are heard do not need to scream. I have photographed all over the world, doing reportage in a wide range of situations, from NGOs in Africa to homes for the elderly in Vienna. Each time I experienced how important it is for people to be recognised, to be listened to with respect and interest – especially for those whose opinions have never been sought or who have never been made the centre of anyone's attention.

A museum, which, according to the International Council of Museums,[2] is 'a permanent institution in the service of society and its development', should aim, in particular, to reach out to those who do not accept the fact that 'we do live nowadays in societies that are pluralistic and there is no way back' (Charim 2018). And ethnographic museums are special places in this regard: they can play an unparalleled role in facilitating openness and acceptance among people in this transition from presumed homogeneity and familiarity into the plural societies in which we now live. They need, however, to first deal with their difficult past of looking at and collecting artefacts of so-called primitive cultures. Only then can they become living 'sites of conscience' in the present day, sites for working through history.

The question, however, is: how should museums take up this role? How might they be places for open encounters between the local and the stranger, the fearful and the feared, without fixing these roles as unchanging or oppositional subjectivities? Technically, this could be achieved by inviting people randomly to participate, to contribute their stories, and to talk about what is important to them; this could materialise in an object they select from the museum or an object they already own. This was the context of *Out of the Box*. Adopting this method could draw new and different people to visit museums, which through their involvement would become a place of their own.

Another option is to bring the museum to the people. I am all for pop-up exhibitions in hospitals in shopping malls or in train stations, confronting audiences with the theme of the place they are in. How has suffering been depicted or denied? In what ways have notions of gender, of masculinity, for example, changed over the last one hundred or three hundred years? How has shopping changed over the centuries? What is the experience of being forced into exile or to flee one's homeland or migrate from one land to another? How did and do we frame some people as belonging and others as outsiders? If a viewer is confronted with the fact that my grandparents or my friends' parents had to leave their country, would that invite empathy and a change of perception? I think it can. Of course some museums have been trying these strategies for some time, even if not always in a progressive manner or with success.

---

2   See https://icom.museum/en/activities/standards-guidelines/museum-definition/.

I think that the only themes that really touch and connect us with others are those that are both personal and universal, those that on one level or another are true for every human being, even if differently so. Marshall Rosenberg[3] and his technique of nonviolent communication had a decisive influence on my approach to photographing people. He argues that people all over the world are driven by a set of basic universal needs such as autonomy, acceptance, community, emotional safety, physical nurturance, play, and respect. Fear and hatred are the result of one of these needs not being met. I think museums need to create exhibitions with universal themes that touch both on an emotional and an intellectual level, opening up to heterogeneity and similarities, instead of foregrounding community or group differences, which inherently emphasises differences between 'us' and 'them'.

5.
I find the concept of 'communities', which interests many ethnographic museums, very questionable. Is it not presumptuous for a museum to 'choose' a community about or with which to make an exhibition if the wish does not come from the community itself? We do have to face the fact that our world is changing, our western societies cannot be classified or explained in terms of communities anymore, and problems cannot be understood or solved by this kind of categorisation. In the plural world we live in today, one's own identity does not come naturally, if it ever did. Instead, increasingly we are required to make decisions about being religious or non-religious, about food, sports, and culture, regardless of where we come from and how long we or our ancestors have lived in the country.

*Out of the Box* has been important for my artistic practice. It has made me realise that I was limiting myself to my own project 'Fremd bin ich gekommen'. I thought that by addressing people with a migrant background, I was working openly, without favouring specific communities. Now I realise that by choosing one group I have been excluding others: those who regard themselves as non-migrants. I realised that at times I too have felt like a stranger in the world, and that suffering from a physical impairment could lead to feelings of outsiderness. And I know from my year-long work with homeless people how much they suffer from not being seen as belonging to our world. I do not need to have a foreign passport or parents born in another country to feel like a stranger. The project has pushed me to expand 'Fremd bin ich gekommen' to non-immigrant Viennese as well. To feel like a stranger, in this way, is a universal theme, even if we are strangers in different ways. To feel like a stranger is much more precarious, even life threatening for some. Not being heard or feeling afraid are subjects that interest me and that are relevant for each and every one of us. There are wonderful objects that can be

---

3   Presented during training session in Vienna in 2017.

used to battle fear in the world, ranging from prayer book to cuddle blanket. These could be a feast for a museum.

I do believe that museums, if they want to make a difference, have to be both *about* something and *for* someone (Weil 1999). They cannot be mere spaces of research, collection and preservation and they do not need to become a place for inappropriate social work. They do have a responsibility that goes further. As the Austrian writer Peter Waterhouse (2018) said in an article for *Falter*, a Viennese weekly journal, when he recently resigned his lifelong membership of the prestigious Austrian Art Senate to protest against the right-wing political programme of our government and their cultural plans: 'There is no such thing as a culture nation (*Kulturnation*) because culture is never national'. Humanity is never national either.

## References

Charim, Isolde. 2018. *Ich und die Anderen*: *Wie die neue Pluralisierung uns alle verändert*. Vienna: Zsolnay Verlag.

Golding, Viv. 2013. 'Collaborative Museums: Curators, Communities, Collections'. In *Museums and Communities: Curators, Collections and Collaboration*, edited by Viv Golding and Wayne Modest, 13-31. London and New York: Bloomsbury.

Gunn, Shirley. n.d. '"The Very Personal Is What Changes People's Consciousness": An Interview with Activist Shirley Gunn'. *International Coalition of Sites of Conscience*. Accessed 1 June 2018. https://www.sitesofconscience.org/en/2018/04/the-very-personal-is-what-changes-peoples-consciousness-an-interview-with-activist-shirley-gunn/.

Iervolino, Serena. 2013. 'Museums, Migrant Communities and Intercultural Dialogue in Italy'. In *Museums and Communities: Curators, Collections and Collaboration*, edited by Viv Golding and Wayne Modest, 113-129. New York: Bloomsbury.

International Council of Museums. n.d. 'Museum Definition'. Accessed 1 June 2018. https://icom.museum/en/activities/standards-guidelines/museum-definition/.

Müller, Wilhelm. 1823. *Die Winterreise*.

Onciul, Bryony. 2013. 'Community Engagement, Curatorial Practice, and Museum Ethos in Alberta, Canada'. In *Museums and Communities: Curators, Collections and Collaboration*, edited by Viv Golding and Wayne Modest, 79-97. New York: Bloomsbury.

Waterhouse, Peter. 2018. 'Seien Sie nicht so verbissen!' *Falter* 14/18, 4 April.

Weil, S. E. 1999. 'From Being about Something to Being for Somebody: The Ongoing Transformation of the American Museum'. *Daedalus* 128, no. 3: 229-258.

Fig. 8.2. *Itai Margula*. Photo by Aleksandra Pawloff for the exhibition *Out of the Box* at Weltmuseum Wien, Vienna.

Fig. 8.3. *Harold Otto*. Photo by Aleksandra Pawloff for the exhibition *Out of the Box* at Weltmuseum Wien, Vienna.

Fig. 8.4. *Sabria Lagoun*. Photo by Aleksandra Pawloff for the exhibition *Out of the Box* at Weltmuseum Wien, Vienna.

Fig. 8.5. *Samira Rauter*. Photo by Aleksandra Pawloff for the exhibition *Out of the Box* at Weltmuseum Wien, Vienna.

Fig. 9.1. CC BY-NC-ND, Photo: Rose-Marie Westling, 2011, Image No 1112.0439. Source: National Museums of World Culture – Etnografiska museet, Sweden, http://collections.smvk.se/carlotta-em/web/object/2157237.

# The Long Walk: Following the Tick-Ticking Sounds into the Unknown – or, The Omitted

JACQUELINE HOÀNG NGUYỄN

> Images are the archive of the collective memory. The twentieth century distinguishes itself from all previous centuries because it has left a photographic trace. What is seen only once and recorded, can be perceived any time and by all. History becomes the shared singularity of an event.
>
> - Susan Buck-Morss

In the fall of 2015, the Swedish National Museums of World Culture in Stockholm and Gothenburg were, for the first time, opening their archives for an artist-in-residence. The residency was positioned within the EU project 'Sharing a World of Creativity, Inclusion, and Heritage' (SWICH), an initiative of ten museums of ethnography and world culture that aimed to develop collaborative and inclusive practices that investigate the potential of shared authority in the museum context. Artists with a diaspora background who could develop historical as well as inventive relations to the archive and its (im)possible futures were encouraged to participate. Amongst more than one hundred applications from all corners of the world, I was selected to be the first artist-in-residence at the Museum of Ethnography in Stockholm. In this short essay, I reflect on some of the challenges of being a guest artist within this institutional context. My presence antagonized the museum's mission and imagined public, in part, I have concluded, because my body carries a history of migration, and one that is tainted by French colonization and American imperialism.

My initial proposal for the residency was to rely on my family's biographical photographs in order to contrast them with similar images in the museum's collections. Photographs belonging to our family came from Indochina during the Nguyễn Dynasty and travelled different journeys from those of comparable images held by the museum. Our photographs endured two wars and had to be smuggled out of Vietnam in 1982, when my grandparents left the war-torn country to join their children in Montreal, Canada, thanks to Vietnam's Orderly Departure Program under the auspices of the United Nations High Commissioner for Refugees. It was not uncommon for former South Vietnamese people to burn their clothes, photographs, and any other traces that could link them to the previous government, the Republic of Vietnam, in fear of recrimination from the new regime. The fact that this small collection of family photographs survived the tumultuous decades is quite noteworthy.

Our family history as migrants, however, like that of many others who also left countries under strenuous situations, has little recognisable cultural value for anyone besides our family and immediate community. The cherished photographs my grandparents brought on the journey could easily have ended up stored in a wardrobe, piling up dust in an attic, damaged in a basement, or, worst of all, lost.

In contrast, museums of ethnography preserve artefacts and photographs in perpetuity in climate-controlled environments. Hypothetically, such images could be of my relatives. Since the Vietnamese language relies predominantly on kinship terminology, it evokes a sense of proximity between Vietnamese viewers and the subjects portrayed, conveying relatedness, at least linguistically. Yet, the actual lives of my possible relatives, the images of whom have been collected in Western museums, and those of their descendants who fled their homes for a better future due to multiple wars, have not been of interest. Photographs brought back from ethnographic expeditions, filed away in the colonial archive, are cared for *ad vitam aeternam*, and the ethnographers celebrated through time for their scientific contributions.

My goal for the residency was to raise two questions: 'How do family histories of migrants, based upon vernacular photography, create friction when put in relation with similar institutional documents?' and 'What type of knowledge is thus constructed between the vernacular and the official documents?' Inserting my non-European body into this Western and modern institution, I felt that my quest and presence worked to bedevil the archive and some of its staff. Historically, these institutions functioned as ivory towers for intellectuals, predominantly white men and their female counterparts who often were relegated to clerical work. Today, when a person of colour, such as myself, is brought into the institution, it is often expected that they will act as a native informant and generate more knowledge for the existing collections, rather than challenge its existing framework.

The SWICH project showed that the 'native informant' role can take many forms. At a workshop held at the Royal Museum for Central Africa in Tervuren, Belgium, in December 2015, one of the participants, an anthropologist, carefully voiced her anxiety about her participation in this project. In addition to her proper academic credentials, she also belonged to a so-called source community for a collection of objects from Southeast Asia. She explained that her host museum had decided to move away from the 'artist-in-residence' model to one featuring an 'expert-in-residence', with the expectation that the visiting scholar would cast more light on the museum's collections. The scholar clearly struggled to determine how she was being positioned within the project and how she and her community at home would benefit from this exchange. If the museum saw her as a native informant, how could their work be a true collaboration?

In my project, the friction between the biographical documents and the museum's collected material, used for 'scientific' endeavour, problematised the museum's universality and raised questions about who the institution serves. Yet, despite my desire to reflect upon the museum's ordering of knowledge, I was left with this conundrum: how would I re-work, re-mediate, translate, interpret, and edit my family history in a way that would not be seen through the 'ethnographic' lens? Faced with the difficulty of the question and resistant to the idea of generating more intellectual capital that would mostly serve the institution, I decided instead to change the course of my investigation and critically explore the mechanisms that enabled collecting practices at the museum.

I embarked on the journey intending to work with Ann Laura Stoler's idea of the archive as subject, rather than object. In her book *Along the Archival Grain: Epistemic Anxieties and Colonial Common Sense* (2009), Stoler suggests, after scrupulously analysing the Dutch archival record, that 'imperial dispositions' and alternating forms of 'epistemic uncertainty and clarity' are buried in archival holdings. For her, rather than using the archive as a privileged and objective source of historical information that is to be extracted from, she treats the archive as a subject in and of itself, demanding of painstaking scholarly attention. I decidedly turned my gaze to the practices of collecting and the making of the institution, rather than reproducing the work of the museum's earlier staff by looking at 'other cultures' and 'other people' as the object of study. With this framework, the residency felt closer to fieldwork *in the museum* than fieldwork *for the museum*, a methodology that Clementine Deliss, former Director of the Museum der Weltkulturen (Museum of the World's Cultures) in Frankfurt am Main, Germany, encouraged her artists-in-residence to adopt.[1]

According to Irene Svensson, ethnographer, social anthropologist and former employee at the Museum of Ethnography in Stockholm, the Swedish museum began its history with the collections of objects that were donated by the Royal Academy of Sciences at its founding in 1739, and thereafter managed the collections. The interest in ethnographica or curiosities, as they were called at the time, increased in the eighteenth century, a time of major scientific expeditions. Sweden's most celebrated explorer, Sven Hedin (1865-1952), who was also a geographer, topographer, photographer, travel writer, and illustrator, contributed extensively to enriching the museum's collections. The extensive holdings of the Hedin Foundation (Sven Hedins Stiftelse) are also to be found in the Museum of Ethnography and in the National Archives in Stockholm. That being said, the foundation is otherwise independent from the museum.

Despite my change of direction – from juxtaposing my family history and the museum's photographic collection to exploring the making of the museum as an institution – my focus remained on photography rather than ethnographic objects. I had the privilege of strolling freely amongst the stacks of photographs in the museum. As time went on, however, I could sense that my presence created internal pressure on the institution. I sometimes worked late in the library, I freely perused the archives where documents and photographs were held, and

---

1   Between 2010 and 2015, Deliss was director of Museum der Weltkulturen (Museum of the World's Cultures) in Frankfurt am Main, Germany, with the aim of initiating a paradigm shift in the museums of ethnography. Whilst centred on the existing collection, the process required reframing, rethinking and reinterpreting objects in the collection by working collaboratively with artists.

I asked questions that were variously informative, productive, or, sometimes, revealing of the oddities of the museum.

I was once cross-examined by an administrator who seemed irritated, to my best guess, by my ease and composure in the museum's backstage. Jacques Derrida and Anne Dufourmantelle (2000) offer helpful insights in *Of Hospitality* on the challenges to be with each other – the stranger, the foreigner, even to the one without a name – where space collapses between distance and extreme proximity. Hospitality retains the trace of hostility, and hostility retains the trace of hospitality. In order to be hospitable, the host must retain some kind of control over the people who are being hosted. Derrida says: 'I want to be master at home, to be able to receive whomever I like there. Anyone who encroaches on my "at home", on my ipseity, on my power of hospitality, on my sovereignty as host, I start to regard as an undesirable foreigner, and virtually as an enemy. This other becomes a hostile subject, and I risk becoming their hostage' (Derrida and Dufourmantelle 2000, 53). During my residency, the museum's physical borders were clear, such as walls, stairs, doors, passes, special keys, hidden keys, and so on. Despite the freedom I had, I could sometimes perceive a certain reluctance if I sought to access particular material. While I entirely understand that museum procedures are in place to ensure the longevity of the collections, and that the understaffed museum could not always accommodate my needs, I sometimes had the sense that the restrictions were enforced by ideological motivations. And this latter impression felt akin to walking on a minefield or wearing a belt made of explosives. Was this feeling conveyed by the staff? Or was it my internalisation of my feeling of non-belonging? Of course it could be both. Still, a feeling of my being an imposter was also very present.

One day, the museum's conservator asked me with a bemused tone to follow him. He might have seemed overbearing, given his large stature and deep voice, but his demeanour had always been friendly. We had not discussed my research in much detail, just the outlines, but I could nonetheless sense that he welcomed my presence in the museum. After the workers' daily three o'clock coffee break, he said: 'Follow me, I have something to show you'. His office, located in the basement, was next to the storage rooms where objects and photographs were kept. So far, I had mostly worked in the upstairs archive room, next to the archivist's office, where boxes of photographs were temporarily kept while she undertook her Herculean task of digitising the photographic archive. An additional storage room was off-site, in a separate house next to the museum, where the nitrate photographs were kept due to their highly flammable chemical content. The cool rooms for long-term preservation were in the basement. Walking down the staircase with the conservator, it felt like descending into the institution's unconscious, where its fears and desires are locked. The conservator had a mischievous sparkle in his eyes and I sensed that I was about to see something unusual – though everything in the museum is already out of the ordinary.

In order to access the vault, keys are kept in different access points, like a treasure hunt. The conservator and I had to walk by ritual masks, poisonous spears, and other objects with various functions and histories. We finally opened a wooden cabinet where a key hung. Once the key was in hand, we retraced our steps until we stood in front of a large door. The key in the keyhole, the door unlocked, he turned the handle and we entered the refrigerated room. The conservator rolled the shelf stacks to the side, and we reached the very back of the room, the last shelving structure. From that shelf, he pulled a burgundy leather-bound object, the size of a thick hardcover book. He slowly opened the box and in it, lay a silver frame adorned with an eagle. I could recognise the emblem of the German Reich. It contained a black and white portrait of Adolf Hitler. At the bottom right corner of the gelatin print, the former German chancellor had hand-written his best wishes to Sven Hedin for his birthday and signed it. The conservator had shown me a forbidden photograph that no one is allowed to see. The object had been omitted in the museum's inventory catalogue, which means it officially does not exist in the museum's collections, and it had deliberately been redacted from Sweden's history. There's the illusion that if nothing is seen, there is nothing there.

In Sweden, it is regularly argued that Sven Hedin was a sympathiser of the Nazi Party, but evidence is always lacking to support this statement. I do not want to take part in that conversation. Rather, I wish to think together with Tina Campt, who encourages us to see beyond images. In her recent book *Listening to Images*, Campt (2017) suggests that sonic vibrations can be used as another mode of contact with images. In other words, images move us in certain ways and create a physical response. Only some frequencies can be heard by the human ear; some are not perceivable. Campt's idea, although never vibrating my eardrum, was like a silent bomb, resounding at subsonic frequencies in me. For me, the portrait in itself is not particularly disturbing, but rather the set of relations it unfolds. The 'amical intimacy' or 'political relations' among all parties involved – its provenance and the familiarity between the sender and the addressee and, more importantly, the institution acting as the custodian of this object – these, to me, make me lose balance. In this face-to-face encounter with Hitler's portrait, I am flooded with many questions: What does it mean, in today's excess of images, that one specific photograph cannot be seen? How many other similar documents or objects have been erased from history, consciously removed from public consciousness? And, more importantly, what is the institution's accountability towards its public with the knowledge it produces and reproduces?

Over the course of the residency, as I became more reluctant to display my family history, I developed a conviction that the museum should continue to welcome people with 'foreign backgrounds' to critically assess the museum's colonial legacy and how it still manifests in today's activities. This, I came to believe, was an important way to challenge how some stories are erased or elided, to illuminate how the making of the museum was partly a making of 'the white gaze'. This term was coined by Swedish art historian Jeff Werner (2014), and he suggests it operates on three levels. First, it points to what is worth drawing attention to about the world, and then to how it is to be represented. Finally, it is blind to its own colour, while being sensitive to the colour of others. In short, the white gaze is a discriminating gaze. I think much of the remaining work for institutions like the Museum of Ethnography is to continue to critically unpack their 'white gaze' and the repercussions of the worldviews this gaze has created before expecting people of colour to come and generate even more knowledge for them. The residency should move beyond generating knowledge that can be further appropriated – as in source community projects – and take up practices of undoing.

About one week before the opening of my exhibition, which resulted from the SWICH residency and additional independent research at the Museum of Ethnography, the communications department kindly asked me to reconsider the expression 'racialised bodies' that I had used in my press release before sending it out to the public, as the institution was clearly uncomfortable with the term. This is a simple example of how institutions such as this one, which have long been central to the construction of racial categories, remain unable, even unwilling, to name and confront the very legacy they have helped to create.

## References

Campt, Tina. 2017. *Listening to Images*. Durham, NC: Duke University Press.

Derrida, Jacques, and Anne Dufourmantelle. 2000. *Of Hospitality*. Translated by Rachel Bowlby. Stanford, CA: Stanford University Press.

Stoler, Ann Laura. 2009. *Along the Archival Grain: Epistemic Anxieties and Colonial Common*. Princeton, NJ: Princeton University Press.

Svensson, Irene. 2012. *Etnografiska Museet: Museihistoria*. https://www.varldskulturmuseerna.se/files/Etnografiska/samlingar/Historik%20-%20Etnografiska%20museet%20och%20arkivet.pdf.

Werner, Jeff. 2014. 'Open Your Eyes to White'. In *Skiascope*, edited by Jeff Werner and Tomas Björk, 33-53. Gothenburg: Gothenburg Museum of Art Publication Series. http://su.diva-portal.org/smash/get/diva2:795315/FULLTEXT01.pdf.

Fig. 9.2. Notebook series 1-3. Genealogy book belonging to Jacqueline Hoàng Nguyễn's private collection. Written by her great-grandfather in Saigon in 1973, and subsequently translated into French by her grandfather in Montreal in 2001, the genealogy book traces the artist's family history back to 1779. Copyright: Jacqueline Hoàng Nguyễn.

Fig. 9.2. Notebook series 1-3. Genealogy book belonging to Jacqueline Hoàng Nguyễn's private collection. Written by her great-grandfather in Saigon in 1973, and subsequently translated into French by her grandfather in Montreal in 2001, the genealogy book traces the artist's family history back to 1779. Copyright: Jacqueline Hoàng Nguyễn.

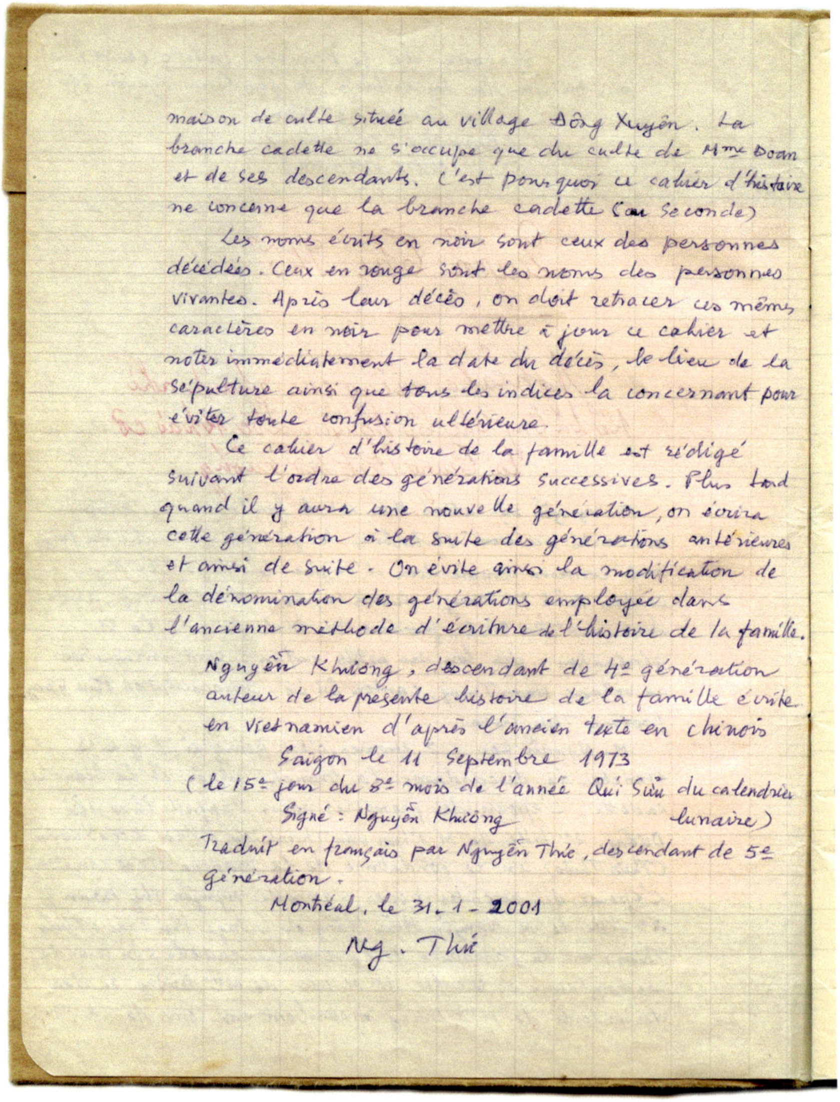

maison de culte située au village Đồng Xuyên. La branche cadette ne s'occupe que du culte de Mme Doan et de ses descendants. C'est pourquoi ce cahier d'histoire ne concerne que la branche cadette (ou Seconde)

Les noms écrits en noir sont ceux des personnes décédées. Ceux en rouge sont les noms des personnes vivantes. Après leur décès, on doit retracer ces mêmes caractères en noir pour mettre à jour ce cahier et noter immédiatement la date du décès, le lieu de la sépulture ainsi que tous les indices la concernant pour éviter toute confusion ultérieure.

Ce cahier d'histoire de la famille est rédigé suivant l'ordre des générations successives. Plus tard quand il y aura une nouvelle génération, on écrira cette génération à la suite des générations antérieures et ainsi de suite. On évite ainsi la modification de la dénomination des générations employée dans l'ancienne méthode d'écriture de l'histoire de la famille.

Nguyễn Khương, descendant de 4e génération auteur de la présente histoire de la famille écrite en vietnamien d'après l'ancien texte en chinois
Saïgon le 11 Septembre 1973
(le 15e jour du 8e mois de l'année Qui Sửu du calendrier lunaire)
Signé : Nguyễn Khương

Traduit en français par Nguyễn Thứ, descendant de 5e génération.
Montréal, le 31.1-2001
Ng. Thứ

Fig. 9.2. Notebook series 1-3. Genealogy book belonging to Jacqueline Hoàng Nguyễn's private collection. Written by her great-grandfather in Saigon in 1973, and subsequently translated into French by her grandfather in Montreal in 2001, the genealogy book traces the artist's family history back to 1779. Copyright: Jacqueline Hoàng Nguyễn.

Fig. 9.3. Photo Album 1. Page from the artist's family photo album. It contains approximately five hundred photographs dated from ca. 1910s to 1974. The main caption in French at the bottom left of the page reads: Here is the birthplace of six generations of the junior branch of the Nguyễn located at No. 6 Street Hồ Xuân Hương, Huế.
The two photos show the house of worship of the ancestors dilapidated following the incursion of the communists in 1968.
The photo opposite represents the newly reconstructed house for the ancestors' worship. But it was sold because all the descendants of the Nguyễns no longer live in Huế.
n.b. Degrees of kinship are indicated in relation to Jackie Hoàng Nguyễn.
Copyright: Jacqueline Hoàng Nguyễn. None of the images from the family collection can be reproduced without the artist's written permission.

# Inclusion

Fig. 10.1. A talk with collaborator Richard Sendi and curator Tina Palaić, 17 January 2018. Photo: Wolfgang Thaler.

# Shared Authority Matters: Collaboration with Heritage Bearers with Migrant Background

TINA PALAIĆ AND BOJANA ROGELJ ŠKAFAR

This paper explores a recent research and exhibition project carried out by the Slovene Ethnographic Museum (SEM) as part of the broader Creative Europe-funded project Sharing a World of Inclusion, Creativity and Heritage (SWICH). The project's focus was on transnational connections that took place between 1960s and 1990s between the former Yugoslavia, especially Slovenia, and various African countries that were members of the Non-Aligned Movement (NAM). More specifically, the focus was on the former Museum of Non-European Cultures, with an emphasis on the stories and collections of Slovenian collectors of the African collections in the care of the museum from that time. We also invited people who came as students from different African countries, remained, and built a career and family in Slovenia to participate in the project. They contributed their memories, experiences, and reflections, as well as brought personal objects from their original countries, which they selected themselves. The results of this project were presented at the exhibition entitled *Africa and Slovenia: A Web of People and Objects*.

In what follows we first sketch the context within which this project happened, tracing briefly SEM's history and the history of the Non-Aligned Movement. We then describe and locate the project theoretically and practically, focusing on SEM's collaboration with the community, before putting forth final thoughts about the importance of this project for ethnographic and world cultures museums today.

### Collecting 'Non-Western' Cultures: A Brief History

SEM is the principal museum of ethnology in Slovenia with both Slovenian and non-European collections presented side by side in the museum's permanent exhibitions.[1] The museum was established to present traditional culture as well as mass and pop culture in Slovenia and the Slovene diaspora, and also to display artefacts from non-European cultures. The first non-European collections were originally part of the Carniolan Provincial Museum established in 1821, and with the formation of independent Ethnographic Museum in 1923 they were joined with the Slovene ethnographic collections. During the Non-Aligned Movement, the Museum of Non-European Cultures was established as a branch of the SEM in 1964[2] in the Goričane castle near Ljubljana and then closed in 2001. Today's SEM also includes the collections gathered within this institution.

Already at its founding as an independent ethnographic museum in 1923, SEM established a strategy for researching, collecting, and presenting the Slovenian

---

1  *Between Nature and Culture* (2006): https://www.etno-muzej.si/en/razstave/between-nature-and-culture,; *We and Others: Images of My World* (2009): https://www.etno-muzej.si/en/razstave/i-we-and-others-images-of-my-world.

2  It operated between 1964 and 2001 when all the collections were transported to SEM and included in the new museological narration based on the museum's re-establishment, which included a new location (as of 1997) as well as a completely new strategy.

ethnological heritage, which guided the work of the museum throughout the twentieth century. No similar strategy existed for the non-European collections, which were to a great extent randomly given a place in the museum, based on the desires of their collectors. It was not until the 1990s that SEM developed a consistent collecting policy, including an in-depth theoretical rationale for non-European collections. These collections, therefore, reflect the affinities, opportunities, and tastes of their collectors, who were missionaries, diplomats, seafarers, and travellers (Rogelj Škafar 1993, 35). They donated or sold the collections and objects to the museum from the mid-nineteenth century onwards.

After the Second World War, numerous objects were transferred to the museum from the Federal Collecting Centre, an organization founded after the war to collect and protect cultural and historical objects for the next central Slovenian museum. A large portion of objects were confiscated from the Bengal Museum, the Peter Claver Society, and individual members of the pre-war nobility.[3] Though fewer in number, ethnologists working in the field also collected objects, including in the 1970s, after visits of the then director Boris Kuhar and curator Pavla Štrukelj to different African countries. It was Kuhar who founded the Museum of Non-European Cultures as a branch of SEM in 1964 (Rogelj Škafar 1993, 45). In the 1980s, the non-European collections were further expanded through the addition of objects collected by Slovenes whose professional careers took them to the so-called Third World.

In the mid-1990s and after Slovenia gained independence, SEM faced the challenge of establishing a modern ethnological museum. Concomitantly, questions started to emerge regarding what to do with the non-European collections. One result of this thinking was the permanent exhibition *Reflections of Distant Worlds*, which presented the attitude of the Slovenes toward non-European cultures and was informed by the collections (Čeplak Mencin, Terčelj, and Frelih 2009, 145-80).

The new millennium saw a shift in the emphasis of the museum's curators. Especially in recent years, there has been a growing awareness about the importance of including the participation of those who were the *carriers of culture* in how these cultures were interpreted. This approach – sharing curatorial or interpretive authority when dealing with non-European collections – has been gradually becoming a common practice in SEM, coinciding with the growing significance of similar practices within the field.

---

3   The Bengal Museum (Ljubljana) and Peter Claver Society (Ljubljana; see Frelih and Koren [2016]) were both missionary organisations that were nationalised due to the changed social situation, and several valuable art and everyday objects were requisitioned from the pre-war nobility as well.

## Non-Aligned Movement: Solidarity, Fraternity, Equality

After the end of World War II, countries across the world experienced political and economic turbulence. This coincided with the time of decolonization, the dismantling of former colonial empires, and the later independence of countries across Africa, Asia, and the Caribbean. In the years that followed, two ideological blocs emerged – Western capitalist and Eastern communist – resulting in tensions that would form the basis of the Cold War. Newly established post-war countries, among them the Socialist Federal Republic of Yugoslavia, were founded under the pressure to join one or the other bloc. Yugoslav president Josip Broz Tito advocated for a neutral position regarding the NATO or Warsaw Pact that became the first pillar of the Non-Aligned policy, followed by the strong demand for the peaceful coexistence of all nations. A decisive moment toward the founding of the Non-Aligned Movement (NAM) was the meeting of African and Asian states in Bandung, Indonesia, in 1955. The conference was an expression of the idea of Afro-Asian unity and included twenty-nine countries from Asia, Africa, and the Middle East, representing a majority of the world's population at the time.

The first NAM conference was held six years later in Belgrade, under the auspices of Yugoslavia. Presidents of Yugoslavia, India, Egypt, Indonesia, and Ghana, and a range of representatives of other African and Asian countries established an international political cooperation to support the fight against imperialism, colonialism, and racism, and advocate for equality, political, and economic cooperation, as well as for territorial sovereignty of all member states. Shortly after the first conference, the movement was joined by the Latin American countries contributing to its worldwide dimension.

In addition to political and economic solidarity within NAM, great importance was given to art and culture.[4] Cultural equality had been established as one of the most important principles of NAM at the Cairo conference in Egypt in 1964. The cultural development of decolonizing countries was foregrounded, and, as Bojana Piškur (2016) has argued, people who were denied their cultural heritage in the past, due to colonialism, started to use its emancipatory potential to tell their own stories. That was done for instance through traveling exhibitions, organized by NAM countries; participation in different cultural events in Western countries; as well as demands for the restitution of artworks that had been taken out of their countries during colonial times and put in various Western museums.

Due to the Non-Aligned policy, Yugoslavia established close collaborations with countries in Africa, the Middle East, and Asia in the fields of politics, economy, and education. Great emphasis was put on cultural exchange. There were at least three spaces in the former Yugoslavia where the material culture of peoples globally was brought together and placed on display: the Museum of Non-European Cultures, as a department of the Slovene Ethnographic Museum in Ljubljana; the Ethnographic Museum in Zagreb; and the Museum of African Art in Belgrade. In those institutions, NAM mem-

---

4   For examples of solidarity in the field of culture and art, see Piškur (2016).

ber states' cultures were represented with many exhibitions and accompanying events that celebrated cultural diversity. The Museum of Non-European Cultures in Ljubljana, the capital city of Slovenia, which was at the time one of the six republics of Yugoslavia, brought together several collections that had been donated or sold by a variety of people, from politicians, businessmen, and journalists to cultural/heritage specialists, who during their various travels purchased or received craft and art objects, as representative of the places they visited. At the same time, Yugoslav scholarships for foreign students enabled many young people from NAM member states to study in Yugoslavia, also at the universities in Slovenia, and they brought their personal objects as well. Some of them donated or sold them to the museum, and they were also involved in many museum events to share knowledge about their cultures (Frelih and Koren 2017, 8-9). Such cultural processes of diplomacy, trade, and exchange occurred up until the dissolution of Yugoslavia in 1990s. None of the former Yugoslav republics, now independent states, are full members of NAM today.

It is within this context of political and cultural exchange that SEM acquired some of its collections of non-European ethnography. Those collections, and the various relations out of which they emerged, formed one of the bases of our project. Limited by the fact that there were not collections to connect to all the project's collaborators who arrived in the '60s, '70s, and '80s from different African countries to study in Slovenia, they were invited to choose personal objects to provide personal narratives for the exhibition.

## Collaboration with Heritage Bearers

The research and collaborative exhibition developed within the framework of this project aimed to explore the transnational connections and exchanges between Yugoslavia and other NAM member states, and especially the museum practices from that time, which to date remain largely unexplored. With the exhibition, the museum presented for the first time complementary perspectives – that of the museum and of the participant 'community' – on non-European collections from the time of NAM. This helped to deepen our understanding of the role and aftermath of this movement, as well as of the collecting practices in the former Museum of Non-European Cultures.

In addition, rising multicultural anxiety in Slovenia (compare Modest and de Koning 2016), which has resulted in increased uneasiness about and fear of migrants in recent years, informed our desire to reflect on the often forgotten openness, friendship, and solidarity among the NAM member states. Although Slovenia is a relatively homogenous society, it is nevertheless also shaped by immigrants and the experiences they bring with them from their 'homeland'. These experi-

Fig. 10.2. Robert Yebuah in his vineyard where curators Bojana Rogelj Škafar and Tina Palaić and photographer Aleš Verbič did a photo shoot with him for the exhibition. Photo: Tina Palaić, 2017.

ences also importantly shape their identity in their new homeland, their feelings of citizenship and affiliation, and their relationships with Slovenes. By addressing the history of NAM, and its role in fashioning a new Slovenian citizenry, we were trying to address the ways that migratory histories are often disconnected with other histories. In short, we wanted to show the contingency of migratory histories.

As authors of this article, and those who spearheaded the collaboration on which the article is based, our aim was to explore and present the personal heritage of African Slovenes[5] in close collaboration with them. The number of African Slovenes from the period of NAM is small[6] (some of them returned to their native countries and others moved to other places), and it is also unbalanced in terms of gender (women in particular moved away).[7] We invited eleven people to cooperate, and five of them responded positively, all of whom were men. They came from different countries of origin with different backgrounds.

Max Zimani moved from Zimbabwe to Slovenia in 1982 to study computer science. Currently, he is the director of the restaurant Skuhna, a world kitchen in the Slovene way, which is a social enterprise that works towards increasing the employability of migrants from Africa, Asia, and South America. Joseph Rakotorahalahy arrived in Slovenia in 1977 from Madagascar. He is an architect and musician. Peter Bossman, who left Ghana in 1977, studied medicine in Yugoslavia and is a renowned physician, and the former mayor of Piran, a tiny coastal town in Slovenia. Richard Sendi moved from Uganda to Slovenia in 1972 to study architecture, and is now employed with the Institute of Urban Planning of the Republic of Slovenia, where he heads Housing Studies. Robert Yebuah came to Slovenia from Ghana in 1965. He studied metallurgy, was employed as a researcher at the Slovene automobile industry, and is currently enjoying his retirement.

As a starting point, our focus was on their shared experience as students in former Yugoslavia. Thereafter, we focused on individual stories and objects. Our exploration of their memories, experiences, and reflections about their education, former student organizations and unions, professional careers, integration into Slovene society, different identifications, cultural exchange, and transnational connections was done jointly as a team, involving both of us and our collaborators (Palaić and Rogelj Škafar 2017a, 45-46). They were not asked to respond to museum collections but to choose personal objects that they either brought with them when they first came to Slovenia or at a later time, following a visit to their native country. The selection criterion was that these objects must be important

---

5    The term was chosen together with our associates as a result of discussion about several options.
6    There is no accurate estimation due to a lack of statistics. On the basis of information gathered through interviews, we estimate there are approximately three hundred people with African heritage living in Slovenia today.
7    When establishing contacts with African Slovenes we got to know only one woman, and she decided not to participate.

Fig. 10.3. Joseph Rakotorahalahy exhibited his mother's handbags: 'These handbags always remind me of her. When I see her objects or pictures, I feel as if she is close to me'. Photo: Aleš Verbič, 2017.

to them, because of their connection with their native country, because they reminded them of some particular event, or simply because they carry a message our collaborators wanted to convey to the museum's visitors. Our collaborators chose personal objects from everyday life that inspired them to talk about their childhood and reflect on their relations with their relatives in their native country; in various situations, some objects help them to express their transnational identity in the Slovene area; and some objects help them to reflect on their values and ideas, including political ones, and represent their culture and native country (Palaić and Rogelj Škafar 2017b, 27).

Our work was based on a participatory research model that advocates for research *with* rather than *about* people (Fluehr-Lobban 2012, 109). This meant that collaborators were involved in determining the research design, methodology, and outcomes of research. Despite some concerns that have emerged in recent years about such approaches, and especially that they represent a threat to the traditional activities of the curator, including collecting, conservation, research, and display (Iervolino 2013, 113), we saw it as an urgent step towards being a more responsive and engaged museum. In our case, sharing curatorial authority was necessary for the credibility of the end results as it both enabled the curators to establish a relationship of trust with collaborators and secondly, it gave collaborators the means to influence the entire process.

More importantly, this approach offered both researchers and collaborators the opportunity to reflect on their assumptions and misconceptions. Didier Fassin (2012, 5, 9) has argued that because research on human activities is always grounded in moral assumptions, a reflexive posture is a necessity. The crucial element of our cooperation was to reconsider the role of all research partners in every phase of the process, and to be open about ethical or difficult questions with our collaborators.

## Epistemic Injustice, Shared Authority, and Radical Transparency

The project advocated for a participatory research model on the basis of three concepts from the field of museum ethics: epistemic injustice, shared authority with heritage bearers, and radical transparency. All of these concepts were closely intertwined in our museum practice. Epistemic injustice results from the exclusion of different social groups from heritage processes, including when their interpretation and understanding of heritage is not taken seriously and considered as valid. That means that the significance of what is transmitted from past to future is distorted. Andreas Pantazatos (2017, 370-71, 375) uses the term 'participant perspective epistemic injustice' to describe this process. Communities that are marginalized by not being provided with the space or opportunity to tell their own story and provide their own interpretation of heritage are excluded from the knowledge economy. To overcome such injustices, external museum partners – communities or individuals – should be seen as competent players in the creation of heritage narratives. In our practice we tried not to reproduce epistemic injustice. This meant engaging in ongoing negotiation about which stories to tell and how they would be exhibited, which played an important role in the collaboration process with African Slovenes. Instead of presenting only the museum's African collections and their collectors, our collaborators were invited to present their personal heritage in the museum environment, which contributed to a more nuanced, in-depth, and comprehensive view regarding the selected topics.

A commitment to shared authority also guided the project. Here we take 'shared authority' to mean those practices aimed at changing entrenched power relations between museum professionals and the audience, still seen in many instances as only consumers and not creators of museum contents. Janet Marstine (2011, 11-12) has argued that shared authority should become a standard practice, especially within ethnographic museums. This approach is important because it directs us to research and represent not just the past of objects but their meaning and value in the present. Shared authority is thus a strategy to address contemporary issues, including socially relevant and challenging issues. Such authority sharing may take three forms: heritage bearers might consult with curators regarding the exhibition content; they might share authority with curators in making decisions about heritage; or a community might use the museum as a place to intervene, addressing societal issues without strong collaboration with museum professionals (Scott 2012, 2-3). In our case, the collaborators accepted responsibility for deciding how information would be shared with the audience. We constantly negotiated the meaning of their heritage and how it should be represented. To avoid the subordination of their voices in both the research and museum exhibition, we together read and critically examined all the texts and images used for the exhibition and accompanying catalogue. By doing this, the lines between us as curators and African Slovenes as collaborators were minimized (see also Fluehr-Lobban 2012, 109).

The concept of radical transparency (Marstine 2011, 14-17) can be applied in the museum environment at multiple levels: within the institution, in relationship with museum stakeholders, and particularly when working with communities or individuals. Most participants in our case expected to be only informants, and they thought that selecting and presenting their heritage was the sole responsibility of the museum. They did not expect that the museum might engage them as equal partners in all the phases. But the structure of the research process was formed together with participants, and they stayed intensely involved during all the phases. It was important to clearly discuss all of our interests, wishes, and expectations regarding the project, and to jointly address questions and dilemmas that emerged. One notable example of such negotiation was a demand by one of our collaborators not to publish a video with stories about his personal objects on SEM's YouTube channel, although videos were an integral part of the exhibition. He argued that a viewer on YouTube was not provided with enough context to truly understand the content of the narrated stories. We decided to include videos only on SEM's website, where the background of the project was thoroughly explained.

## Community, Diaspora, or Something Else?

When we wanted to find a suitable category to describe project participants, whether 'African community' or 'diaspora', we faced the difficulty of using such terms. We agree with museologists Leontine Meijer-van Mensch and Peter van Mensch (2015, 92) who argue that the term 'community' is a social construct, strongly connected to power relations. Defining the community might lead to establishing control over a group of individuals instead of strengthening shared authority with heritage bearers. Especially in the context of migrant belonging, cultural differences are often used as labels of collective identity. Culture might become a tool for division and thus a mechanism for legitimizing social exclusion, a governmentalizing of inclusion (we include you if you behave the way we think members of your community should behave).

We opened up this question to our collaborators, who rejected being recognized as a community or group and preferred to be presented as individuals. Therefore, we agreed to avoid such categorizations and instead present the story of each individual separately, as well as to emphasize their personal memories, decisions, experiences, and reflections. We highlighted some common issues, for instance migration to Yugoslavia, education, involvement in African organizations, and career development, and then presented diverse stories unfolding around these common themes. Despite the fact that they did not want to be recognized as part of the African community or diaspora – they did not feel mandated to speak on behalf of a community – all of them expressed some concern about how the exhibition would represent them and what consequences that might have for other migrants in Slovenia. One of the collaborators clearly stated that the exhibition, which was the first of its kind in SEM (and also in Slovenia), would leave a mark on the people involved and on other migrants with African heritage, and because of that he involved himself even more actively in the exhibition-making processes.

We also had difficulties using the term 'African', which we considered inappropriate for two reasons. First, the African continent is heterogeneous and its countries have different histories, political and economic systems, traditions, etc. Second, all the participants have lived in Slovenia for at least thirty years and have (also) Slovenian citizenship. Based on our conversations about their identifications, we all decided on the name 'African Slovenes' for use in exhibition and catalogue texts. However, in our opinion, more appropriate names would be 'Ghanaian Slovene', 'Ugandan Slovene', 'Zimbabwean Slovene', and 'Malagasy Slovene' (see also Palaić and Rogelj Škafar 2017b, 26-27). This conclusion is based on the self-understanding of our collaborators. One of them claims that 'back home' he was proud of his nationality, and after migrating to Yugoslavia he developed his African identity more because Africans in Yugoslavia dealt with common challenges that provided a basis for their unity. However, he sees himself also as part Yugoslav because he lived in former Yugoslavia, and also as part Slovene because he has lived in independent Slovenia for twenty-seven years. He advocated for multiple identities. Another, for instance, said that he is Slovenian by choice, but at the same moment he also claimed that he cannot be anything but African. Although integrated, he said, your identity stays with you. The other three all expressed that Slovenia is their home now mostly because they built families there. In two cases, the identifications related to their native countries remain strong. This is perhaps due to the ingrained perceptions about national identity in Slovene society. As one of them explained, a person is allowed to claim that he or she is a Slovene citizen, but from the Slovene perspective they are still considered Ghanaian, Ugandan, or Malagasy with a new (or additional) document.

## The Meaning of the Project for the Further Vision of SEM

The themes addressed by the SWICH project were the basis for deep reflection and research, and eventually for an exhibition that addressed complementary perspectives on non-European collections from the time of NAM. This resulted in a deepening of our understanding of SEM's practices as an ethnographic museum, and in particular what it means to collaborate with communities (even though we remain critical of the term). This also allowed for a novel way to address the relationship between objects and people, both carriers of cultures. The project helped us develop a model for social relevance, for cooperation between the museum and citizens. It is a model based on exploring and understanding the social status and role of individuals with migrant backgrounds in relation to objects that also migrated. The conversations that took place around the exhibition were an important intervention in contemporary discussions of migrants, which are often marked by discourses of hate, xenophobia, and anxiety. These discussions helped raise awareness among museum audiences about the diversity of migration trajectories and processes, how histories shape our present, and the contribution of migrants to the development of society. We hope that the collaborative approach we developed in this project inspires other curators in their own collaborative projects with different groups in society, not only at SEM but also other museums that have non-European collections. These collections can be the starting point for developing dialogue across difference and mutual understanding about our shared humanity.

## References

Čeplak Mencin, Ralf, Mojca Terčelj, and Marko Frelih. 2009. 'Reflections of Distant Worlds'. In *Between Nature and Culture: A Guide to the Slovene Ethnographic Museum Permanent Exhibition*, edited by Nena Židov, 145-80. Ljubljana: Slovene Ethnographic Museum.

Fassin, Didier. 2012. 'Introduction: Toward a Critical Moral Anthropology'. In *A Companion to Moral Anthropology*, edited by Didier Fassin, 1-17. Malden, MA: Wiley Blackwell.

Fluehr-Lobban, Carolyn. 2012. 'Anthropology and Ethics'. In *A Companion to Moral Anthropology*, edited by Didier Fassin, 103-14. Malden, MA: Wiley Blackwell.

Frelih, Marko, and Anja Koren. 2016. *Odmevi Afrike: Družba sv. Petra Klaverja za afriške misijone in njeno delovanje v Ljubljani v prvi polovici 20. stoletja* [Echoes of Africa: The St. Peter Claver Society for African Missions and its activities in Ljubljana in the first half of the 20th century]. Stična: Muzej krščanstva na Slovenskem.

Frelih, Marko, and Anja Koren. 2017. 'The Non-Aligned Movement: A Period That Provided the Opportunities for the Origin of African Collections in Slovenia'. In *Africa and Slovenia: A Web of People and Objects*, edited by Bojana Rogelj Škafar, 7-9. Ljubljana: Slovene Ethnographic Museum.

Iervolino, Serena. 2013. 'Museums, Migrant Communities, and Intercultural Dialogue in Italy'. In *Museums and Communities: Curators, Collections and Collaboration*, edited by Viv Golding and Wayne Modest, 113-29. London: Bloomsbury.

Marstine, Janet. 2011. 'The Contingent Nature of the New Museum Ethics'. In *The Routledge Companion to Museum Ethics: Redefining Ethics for the Twenty-first Century Museum*, edited by Janet Marstine, 3-25. Abingdon: Routledge.

Mensch, Peter van, and Leontine Meijer-van Mensch. 2015. *New Trends in Museology II*. Celje: Muzej novejše zgodovine Celje in ICOM Slovenija.

Modest, Wayne, and Anouk de Koning. 2016. 'Anxious Politics in the European City: An Introduction'. *Patterns of Prejudice* 50, no. 2: 97-108.

Palaić, Tina, and Bojana Rogelj Škafar. 2017a. 'Slovenski Afričani: o njihovih osebnih predmetih v prepletu identitet' [African Slovenes: About their personal objects and intertwined identities]. *Etnolog* 27, no. 78: 39-63.

Palaić, Tina, and Bojana Rogelj Škafar. 2017b. 'Slovenski Afričani: o njihovih predmetih v prepletu identitet' [African Slovenes: About their personal objects and intertwined identities]. In *Africa and Slovenia: A Web of People and Objects*, edited by Bojana Rogelj Škafar, 24-47. Ljubljana: Slovene Ethnographic Museum.

Pantazatos, Andreas. 2017. 'Epistemic Injustice and Cultural Heritage'. In *The Routledge Handbook of Epistemic Injustice*, edited by Ian James Kidd, Jose Medina, and Gaile Pohlhaus, Jr., 370-385. New York: Routledge.

Piškur, Bojana. 2016. *Solidarity in Arts and Culture: Some Cases from the Non-Aligned Movement*. http://www.internationaleonline.org/research/alter_institutionality/78_solidarity_in_arts_and_culture_some_cases_from_the_non_aligned_movement.

Rogelj Škafar, Bojana. 1993. *Slovenski etnografski muzej – sprehod skozi čas in le delno skozi prostor = The Slovene Ethnographic Museum – a journey through time and only partly through space = Le Musée éthnographique slovène – promenade à travers le temps et en partie à travers l'espace*. Ljubljana: Slovene Ethnographic Museum.

Rogelj Škafar, Bojana. 2003. 'Etnološki muzeji in nacionalna identiteta: Slovenski etnografski muzej' [Ethnological museums and national identity: Slovene ethnographic museum]. *Etnolog* 13, no. 64: 31-57.

Scott, Katherine Mary. 2012. 'Engaging with Pasts in the Present: Curators, Communities, and Exhibition Practice'. *Museum Anthropology* 35, no. 1: 1-9.

Fig. 11.1. 'Ikunde. Barcelona, Colonial Metropolis', Ethnological and World Cultures Museum, Barcelona. Copyright Museu Etnològic i de Cultures del Món. Ajuntament de Barcelona.

# Uncomfortable Memory and Community Participation at the Barcelona Ethnological and World Cultures Museum

SALVADOR GARCÍA ARNILLAS AND LLUÍS-JOSEP RAMONEDA AIGÜADÉ

## Introduction

This paper analyses some of the exhibitions produced by the Barcelona Ethnological and World Cultures Museum, in collaboration with several communities of African migrants whose cultures of origin are represented in its collections, as well as other exhibitions that offer a critical approach to the museum's colonial past. These projects further explore the social function of the museum through community participation in the creation of a museum voice and through a critical re-evaluation of both museum and city history.

## Founding the Ethnological and World Cultures Museum

The Ethnological and World Cultures Museum is a municipally owned museum run by the Barcelona Institute of Culture. This museum has its origins in two separate institutions founded in the 1940s: the Museum of Popular Industries and Arts (1942), which focused on the traditional and popular culture of Catalonia and the rest of Spain, and the Ethnological and Colonial Museum (1949), dedicated to the cultures of so-called primitive peoples. These institutions underwent several phases of unification and separation throughout their histories, including one most recently (2004-2012) during which they were merged to create the Ethnological Museum of Barcelona. This museum thus held both European and non-European collections, a diversity that allowed it to break with the conventional dichotomy of 'us and the other' that normally organises ethnographic museums. Then, in 2012, the Museum of World Cultures was founded, bringing together private collections with the holdings of the Ethnological Museum of Barcelona (Barcelona City Council 2012).

The Ethnological and World Cultures Museum is, therefore, an umbrella institution merging two disciplinary traditions and two museums into one institution. The first, the World Cultures Museum, which opened in 2015, and whose permanent exhibition displays the diversity of various cultures from Africa, Asia, America, and Oceania, was organised from a World Art perspective. The second, organised through a lens of ethnology, was the Barcelona Ethnological Museum; its permanent exhibition, which was refurbished in 2015, reflects on contemporary society through its ethnological collections from Catalonia and the rest of Spain.

In May 2015, after the municipal elections that resulted in a change in the city government, it was decided to bring together the two institutions. This eventually occurred in 2016, but two sites were maintained. Bringing both European and non-European ethnology together in a single institution offered possibilities for overcoming ethnocentric differentiation.

## Recent Museological Changes

From the beginning, the process to develop the World Cultures Museum (2012-2015) adopted a model of ethnographic objects as art, along the lines of the Musée du Quai Branly in Paris. As in the Paris case, controversy soon emerged surrounding the Barcelona project. Initially, questions were raised about the economic opportunities the project could provide for the city's agenda. Due to the economic crisis at the time, concerns were soon raised about the investment required for such an ambitious project. Very shortly after, the museological approaches adopted by the project were also criticised, as well as the decision to divide the Ethnological Museum collections.

In 2016, a committee of experts was established, comprising anthropologists, university professors, and researchers from the Spanish National Research Council, that 'conceptually' redirected the newly merged institution. This new direction began with a renewed mission to ground the museums' work more in academic anthropology as well as within the city. For practical purposes, it meant centring the city in the museum's narrative, instead of the territories of Catalonia and the rest of Spain, which were the traditional ethnological frameworks in the earlier Museum of Popular Industries and Arts. The mission assigned by this commission of experts is 'the integral management of the ethnological heritage of the city of Barcelona', understood as:

> all those objects, places and material or immaterial manifestations that constitute witnesses and contribute to explain the ways of life of the city, in all its expressions and changes throughout time and in all its diversity and provenance, but always from a contemporary perspective, . . . including those ethnological elements of diverse origin that, whether or not organized in collections, have been deposited in the city of Barcelona. (Committee of experts 2016, 3)

At the time of the merger, a newly completely art exhibition (based on ethnological objects) was at the old World Cultures Museum, which was in tension with the museum's new direction. To resolve this tension, it was decided to use temporary exhibitions at both sites to foreground the new emphasis on the urban, social, and anthropological contextualisation[1] of the collections.

Anthropology museums have adopted many renovation strategies over the last few decades, with aestheticizing anthropological objects as works of art arguably being one of the most powerful strategies. Other strategies have employed objects to reflect critically on controversial issues, or promoting cultural diversity by posing questions about migrant belonging (Van Geert, Urtizberea, and Roigé 2016). In addition to different events and activities, through the temporary exhibitions

---

1  For an analysis of the museological direction of the World Cultures Museum, see Roigé (2015).

programme of the Ethnological and World Cultures Museum there is a strategy we could describe as 'uncomfortable memory exhibitions', which tries to tackle the problems of incorporating alternative perspectives on its collection and to reflect on the complexity of cultural diversity in our times. Even though we have other kinds of exhibitions, this strategy is aimed at converting the space into a social and participatory museum, promoting critical reflection on the role of colonialism in the museum's history and fostering the integration of cultural diversity into its programmes. The programmes dedicated to Africa in recent years and the structural changes at the Barcelona Ethnological and World Cultures Museum reveal a combination of institutional reforms, the application of uncomfortable memory exhibitions, and efforts to increase community participation.

## Looking Critically at Its Colonial Past – *Ikunde: Barcelona, Colonial Metropolis*

The first exhibition planned for the new and unified museum was the exhibition *Ikunde: Barcelona, Colonial Metropolis*, which highlighted Barcelona's role as a colonial metropolis in relation to the African populations of Equatorial Guinea. This exhibition sought to rethink colonial memory, emphasising the ideological selection of colonial facts, and to awaken awareness of the colonial dimensions of Barcelona and Catalan society.

'Ikunde' refers to the Ikunde reception and acclimatisation centre for animals, which was located about 2 km from Bata, in the Rio Muni area of mainland Equatorial Guinea. It was promoted by Barcelona Zoo, set up in 1961, and sponsored by the Barcelona City Council. Besides awakening the colonial memory of Barcelona and Catalonia, the choice of this previously unexplored side of our collective memory questioned the ethnological museum as a site for knowledge production and representation. Indeed, apart from the municipal character of both the museum and the Ikunde centre, the creation in 1949 of the Ethnological and Colonial Museum, one of the two museums that would later become the Ethnological Museum of Barcelona, was directly related to the Equatorial Guinea expedition sponsored by the Institute of African Studies, an agency of the Spanish National Research Council, which was the main Spanish institution promoting research in Spain's colonial possessions (Calvo 1997, 177). Ikunde and the museum, then, were entangled parts of Spain's colonial relation with Africa, parts that are often kept apart.

An analysis of the colonial role played by Catalan and Spanish society more generally is still lacking in Spain's educational system; this perspective has not received much critical treatment[2] in the 'narratives' built around Barcelona or Catalonia, although we can find myriad references in academic literature, especially with regard to the slave

---

2   Except the odd example, such as the documentary film *Guinea Ecuatorial, memoria negra* (Equatorial Guinea, black memory), directed by Xavier Montanyà (2007, 93 min, VOSE), and the Centre de Cultura Contemporània de Barcelona screening and roundtable discussion with Gustau Nerin, José Luis Nvumba, and Xavier Muntanyà.

trade. In this respect, the exhibition highlighted the strong ties that the Catalan capital, beginning with the City Council, had with the Spanish colony of Equatorial Guinea and added a contrast to the artistic perspective of the permanent exhibition.

Initially, the *Ikunde* temporary exhibition,[3] which was small, did not opt for a participatory model, but instead for an anthropological one, together with a research group – the Observatory of Everyday Life – that had a track record in the critical analysis of Catalan and Barcelona society. The University of Barcelona research group on exclusion and social controls also took part.

*Ikunde* showed the human and ecological exploitation of the colony, the destruction of local lifestyles, and ecological depletion. Several sections of the exhibition were intended to address the treatment of and ideas about people and specimens. This informed the choice of objects, 172 in total, that included 42 pieces from the museum, mostly spears, weapons, and carved wooden figures (various Eyema Byeri), as well as animal specimens, in order to explain the inseparable character of the colonial plunder: the human, social, and environmental exploitation of the territory.

One notable feature of the exhibition was the presence of naturalised specimens or parts of specimens, mainly on loan from the Natural Science Museum, also a municipal institution, as well as graphic and printed materials, posters, books, magazines, and enlarged photographs. This was an attempt to show colonial entanglement across scientific disciplines and therefore across object categories. The exhibition's guiding thread was Snowflake, the white gorilla, who was Barcelona Zoo's 'international star' and the basis of a large part of the city's tourist advertising, and who became a genuine attraction and a highly symbolic icon for the city's inhabitants. The exhibition had nine sections: 'Snowflake', Equatorial Guinea as a Spanish colony, three sections on the plunder of live specimens (and dead ones), Claretian missionaries, Barcelona as a metropolis, the role of photography in colonialism, and, finally, postcolonial repercussions in Barcelona.

The exhibition programme included projects that explored 'reflexive' and 'conflictive memory'. There was a 'reference catalogue' developed on the exhibition themes, various audiovisual compilations of archival images, and an extensive programme with sixteen activities (talks, workshops, debates, and screenings), ending with the presentation of a book-sized exhibition catalogue.

In the case of the *Ikunde* exhibition, there was no 'contact zone' created to invite communities of African origin to be involved in preparing the exhibition programme, in contrast with other exhibitions that had been held at the Barcelona Ethnological Museum. However, the discourse in *Ikunde*, which was produced and

---

3   The temporary exhibition room measured 182.79 m², which limited the size of Ethnological and World Cultures Museum temporary exhibitions as it precluded large formats. The small format was not the preference of the programmers.

curated by specialists and academics, clearly moved towards uncomfortable and controversial memories, tackling not only the complexity of Barcelona's history but also of the museum itself, in stark contrast with the 'friendly' perspectives of previous exhibition programmes on Africa. The fact that *Ikunde* firmly opted for a decolonising and self-critical narrative may be related to the 'inter-organisational interference processes' described by Camille Mazé, Frederic Poulard, and Christelle Ventura (2013) in their analysis of institutional change for the transformation of French ethnology museums since 2006.

## *Dialogues with Africa*: Integrating Cultural Diversity and Community Participation into the Museum

When the proposal came to be part of the 'Sharing a World of Inclusion, Creativity and Heritage' (SWICH) project,[4] it was suggested that the Ethnological and World Cultures Museum should be the work-group leader of the 'Diaspora Objects' activity for the topic 'Connecting Diasporas of Objects and Peoples'. The museum team believed that working with the African collections would allow the museum to build on previous participatory experiences with migrant communities, as well as bring together in a joint project museum staff and people from different African communities in Barcelona. An earlier museum participation project that had been done in connection with the European Year of Intercultural Dialogue in 2008 provided a reference point. The Barcelona Ethnological Museum and the Archaeological Museum of Catalonia undertook a joint project called 'Africas'. This involved two exhibitions at the museums with complementary focal points: *The Gaze from the West*, with an archaeological focus, sited at the Archaeological Museum of Catalonia, approached the African continent from the perspective of Europeans' 'fascination' for the continent, while *Journey to the Other Shore*, with an ethnological focus and sited at the Barcelona Ethnological Museum, tackled this journey from the opposite direction, that is, the migratory experience of many Africans coming to Europe.

A group of African migrants helped with the exhibition at the Barcelona Ethnological Museum. They conceived four displays, enriching the exhibition with personal testimonies. Three people's imaginations of their countries of origin were reconstructed through their own experiences, particularly family life, their memories of childhood, the importance of marriage for most women from the Maghreb, and the important role of women in clans in sub-Saharan Africa. The fourth display case was created by a group of migrants who came from Mauritania and were liv-

---

4   SWICH was an EU-funded project that ran from November 2014 to September 2018, in which ten European partner museums reflected current issues concerning the role of ethnographic museums within an increasingly differentiated European society.

ing in Mollet del Vallès, a city close to Barcelona, to show what their country means to them. In their own words and as part of their claim to self-representation, they said that this version of their story did not coincide with that normally presented in 'big institutions' or bear any relation to everyday stereotypes circulating within society. In fact, they said, their display showed a 'Mauritania seen through the eyes of a group of Mauritanians from the Selibaby area', a statement foregrounding the partiality of their view and personal experiences (Fornes and Izquierdo 2008).

The 'Dialogues with Africa' project was conducted throughout 2016 at the World Cultures Museum and involved a focus group, a lab meeting, and a collaborative exhibition. This project was the result of the collaboration between two researchers from the Study Group on Indigenous and Afro-American Cultures at the University of Barcelona, who were working with Catalans originally from Africa, and with the Ethnological and World Cultures Museum.

Six people were invited to take part in the focus group, which met for three sessions. They had links with North Africa, West Africa, and Central Africa, and were chosen intersectionally, according to criteria of gender and ethnic diversity. The aims of the group were to identify the concerns and sensitivities of the three collaborating African communities chosen regarding the museum collections and the representation of their cultures; to collectively reflect on representations, ideas, and memories of Africa through personal objects and museum objects; to foster dialogue between the museum and the communities through objects; and, finally, to strengthen the communities' ties with the city and its institutions, creating a joint space for reflection and memory.[5] At the sessions, each participant presented two objects that brought back memories of their country of origin, while the museum did the same with objects in its collections from the relevant geographical area. Each presentation involved a dialogue between all the participants, with their personal stories and experiences, as well as the objects themselves, jogging the memories of the other participants. After the presentation of the museum objects, the African participants contributed information about them from their own knowledge and personal stories (Celigueta and Izard 2016, 10).

On the basis of the exchange that took place in the three focus group sessions, the researchers from the University of Barcelona drew some conclusions that we highlight below. First, they believe some of the objects brought by the participants (djellabas, dates, pumpkins, etc.) have a great capacity for representing the collective dimension of a cultural tradition, while also giving meaning to the personal stories of their owners, which often tie in with the importance of the family for transmitting culture. Second, they show the difference between personal heritage, linked to a collective memory, and the museum's heritage, which is the product of

---

5   https://www.barcelona.cat/museu-etnologic-culturesmon/montjuic/ca/dialegs-amb-africa (Last accessed 8 April 2019).

Fig. 11.2. 'Dialogues with Africa', Ethnological and World Cultures Museum, Barcelona. Copyright Museu Etnològic i de Cultures del Món. Ajuntament de Barcelona.

external research and scientific appropriation that seeks to be representative of a cultural tradition. Whether these efforts are successful or not must be questioned, as made clear during the sessions when the participants did not recognise the representative nature of some museum objects (Celigueta and Izard 2016, 11).

The 'Dialogues with Africa' project was enriched by the experience of the lab meeting, with participation from the Luigi Pigorini National Museum of Prehistory and Ethnography in Rome, the Royal Museum of Central Africa in Tervuren, and the Weltmuseum Wien. It was a meeting/laboratory designed to share experiences from projects that tried to explore the connections between members of local diasporas and museum collections. The project also benefited from access to some of the stories and objects linked to the dialogue among the researchers, Catalan Africans, and museum professionals.

The third activity linked to the project was the collaborative exhibition *Dialogues with Africa*, which intended to 'create a space of dialogue, reflection and memory' and to 'broaden the spectrum of the museum to reach people who may feel they have been transported to their countries of origin, their roots and their memories' (Izard and Celigueta 2016, 9). The objects owned by individuals and the museum shared a large display case at the museum entrance, and there was also a video for the stories associated with each. This was part of the exhibition's focus as the discourse associated with these items did not arise from scientific knowledge, but was fundamentally rooted in the life stories, memories, and emotions of their owners. But what, then, is the narrative of the museum professionals whose objective is to study its collections? How does a personal narrative fit with scientific discourse? Should there be some differentiation in the museographical treatment of objects that belong to the museum collection and, therefore, are assets that form part of municipal public heritage, and that of objects brought directly from an individual's home? Does 'shared authority' mean just shared showcases, or shall we expect more from this critical concept? Terms such as 'polyvocality', 'shared authority', and 'social inclusion' have become common to contemporary museum theory and practice. They, however, develop a new meaning when the museum tries to put them into practice and comes up against the challenges they imply for museographical praxis.

While the narratives and objects exhibited shared a single display case, the participants of African origins were also visible because there were photographs of them wearing or carrying the objects in question. In contrast, those from the museum were not accompanied by any images of the museum professionals. Perhaps this is a mere, insignificant detail, or perhaps it exemplifies the distance that the museum usually adopts when approaching its collections from a (supposed) 'neutral' perspective, along with the conceptual distance between a sterile interpretation of an object and a personal story that gives life to it.

These participatory experiences enable us to reflect on our interpretive focuses of the collection, and on the supposedly universal and neutral voice we use in the texts and labels in our display cases. In fact, in this exhibition, the museum text is impersonal and uses scientific language to talk about objects in the collection, while the texts describing the items belonging to Catalans of African origin are quotes taken from their own personal testimonies.

## Conclusions

The unification of the Ethnological and World Cultures Museum has involved some changes in the museum's narrative through a complementary programme of temporary exhibitions addressed at compensating for the absence of the ethnological contextualisation in one of its permanent exhibitions. In this paper we have underlined two activities linked with the museum's African collection: the *Ikunde: Barcelona, Colonial Metropolis* exhibition and the 'Dialogues with Africa' project.

The *Ikunde* exhibition's narrative included uncomfortable aspects of colonialism and proposed not only a necessary critical, contextual, and ethnological narrative but also a reorientation to the city of Barcelona. The tensions between different narratives in a context of institutional changes were evident and arguably have enriched the museum's ethnological framework.

The 'Dialogues with Africa' project was conceived as a participatory community project to create and reinforce the links between migrant communities and the museum. We should humbly recognise that, although the museum tries to move alongside the migrants living in Barcelona who come from the countries from which the collections originate, it still has a long way to go. Dialogue and the honest exchange of ideas and experiences will help it become a museum that can truly call itself social and participatory.

## References

Antebi, Andrés, Pablo González, Alberto López, and Eloy Martín, eds. 2017. *Ikunde: Barcelona, Metròpoli Colonial*. Barcelona: Ajuntament de Barcelona, Institut de Cultura, Museu Etnològic de Barcelona.

Barcelona City Council. 2012. 'Creació del nou Museu de Cultures del Món'. Mesura de govern, Consell plenari Municipal, 26 October.

Calvo, Luis. 1997. 'África y la Antropología española: la aportación del Instituto de Estudios Africanos'. *Revista de Dialectología y Tradiciones populares* 52, no. 2: 169-185.

Celigueta, Gemma, and Gabriel Izard. 2016. 'Grups focals: els objectes com a connectors'. In *Diàlegs amb Àfrica: La memòria dels objectes*, Museu de Cultures del Món, 10-11. Barcelona: Institut de Cultura de Barcelona.

Committee of Experts. 2016. 'Un museu per al segle XXI: Conclusions de la comissió per a l'anàlisi i definició estratègica del MEB i el MCM'. Unpublished internal document, June.

Fornés i Garcia, Josep, and Pere Izquierdo, dirs. 2008. Àfriques. Barcelona: Museu d'Arqueologia de Catalunya.

Izard, Gabriel, and Gemma Celigueta. 2016. 'El Museu i el projecte "Diàlegs amb Àfrica"'. In *Diàlegs amb Àfrica. La memòria dels objectes*, Museu de Cultures del Món, 8-9. Barcelona: Institut de Cultura de Barcelona.

Mazé, Camille, Fréderic Poulard, and Christelle Ventura. 2013. 'Démantèlements, reconversions, créations. Contribution à l'analyse du changement institutionnel'. In *Les musées d'ethnologie: culture, politique et changement institutionnel*, edited by Camille Mazé, Frédéric Poulard, and Christelle Ventura, 19-33. Paris: Éditions du Comité des travaux historiques et scientifiques.

Roigé, Xavier. 2015. 'Los museos etnológicos en Cataluña: perspectivas, retos y debates'. *Revista Andaluza de Antropología* 9: 76-104. http://www.revistaandaluzadeantropologia.org/uploads/raa/n9/roige.pdf

Van Geert, Fabien, Iñaki Arrieta Urtizberea, and Xavier Roigé. 2016. 'Los museos de antropología: del colonialismo al multiculturalismo. Debates y estrategias de adaptación ante los nuevos retos políticos, científicos y sociales'. *OPSIS* 16, no. 2: 342-60.

Fig. 12.1. *Diaspora Objects: Reconnections.* Alessya Prawita Dewi Agus and the kris. Copyright: Museo delle Civiltà.

# *The Making of a Point of View*: A Participatory Exhibition at the Pigorini Museum in Rome

ROSA ANNA DI LELLA AND LORETTA PADERNI

## Introduction

Over the last ten years, the Ethnographic Section of the Museo Preistorico Etnografico L. Pigorini[1] has attempted to transform its practices through a series of initiatives that embrace public consultations, co-creation workshops, and participative exhibitions. With the aim of transforming the museum space into a contact zone (Clifford 1997), various projects that experiment with inclusive practices and reflect on the social role of ethnographic museums have been carried out (Sandell 2002).

The exhibition [S]*oggetti migranti: People Behind the Things* was a pivotal moment in the process of renewing how 'otherness' was represented and framed through ethnographic collections (Lattanzi 2012). Realised in the framework of the project READ-ME II[2] (2010-2012), the exhibition aimed at proposing new opportunities for interpreting cultural heritage, by working with different diaspora communities in a participatory process of content coproduction. In this project, the representatives of five diaspora associations were actively involved in the design of the final exhibition. Following this experience, other initiatives were carried out to further expand and deepen the museum's experience with collaborations and to avoid the ever-present risk of creating incidental participative practices and relationships around temporary projects[3]. These participatory projects included the 'Al Museo con' project, which was carried out in 2013-2014 with the aim of increasing audience access and participation in the interpretation of the museum's heritage. The main outcome of this project was a web application that includes six museum trails, each containing a unique narrative (Lattanzi 2014; Lattanzi and Di Lella 2016).

The most recent collaborative activity the Pigorini museum carried out was the exhibition *The Making of a Point of View: Spotlights on the Indonesian and Malaysian Collections*.[4] The exhibition was one the outcomes of a collaboration with a wide network of institutions, individuals, and communities. The process produced four

---

1    In 2016, The Museo Preistorico Etnografico L. Pigorini was merged into the Museo delle Civiltà, a new institution that itself resulted from the joining of three other national museums dedicated to Italian folk cultures (the Museo delle arti e tradizioni popolari), the Oriental arts (the Museo d'arte orientale 'G. Tucci'), and the Middle Ages (the Museo dell'alto medioevo).

2    The project 'Réseau européen des Associations de la Diasporas & Musées d'Ethnographie – READ-ME II' (2010-2012) aimed to re-examine our cultural background and that of the diaspora through direct encounter with the Museum's collection and by comparing, with the representatives of diaspora associations, the contemporary value of ethnographic objects. Pigorini Museum assumed the role of lead museum in the project, while the Musée Royal de l'Afrique Centrale in Tervuren, Musée du Quai Branly in Paris and the Museum für Volkerkunde in Wien became the associate partners.

3    Such practices have already received significant criticism, for the ad hoc nature in which they occur, where inclusion is not taken as core museum practice but is done only when extra money is available. See, for example, Iervolino (2013).

4    The exhibition was part of the *Sharing a World of Inclusion, Creativity and Heritage (SWICH)* project.

installations that served as different points of view on the museum's heritage by staging various ways of presenting objects collected during nineteenth-century geographical explorations, and including the languages of contemporary art, autobiographical narration, and the historical and museographic approach.

This essay explores part of the collaborative process that led to this exhibition, focussing on some of the challenges that emerged while making two of the four installations: *Diaspora Objects: Reconnections* and *Object in Transit: Transformations*, both of which were co-created with a transcultural curatorial group of young adults and teenagers.[5]

## About the Project: Theoretical and Methodological Background

The participative process started at the end of 2015 and lasted until the opening of the exhibition in February 2018. One of our main aims was to promote an exchange of expertise and approaches within a wide network including other institutions, art galleries, diaspora associations, and under-represented groups. We wanted to create multiple 'engagement zones' (Onciul 2013, 84), each one tailored to the participants, and characterised by a variety of approaches and methodologies. Our objective was to integrate two activities that formed part of the SWICH project – the artistic residency and the collaborative exhibition – while expanding the exchange between the museum's staff, the artist in residence H. H. Lim, and the diaspora communities involved in the project.

We decided to develop co-creation activities around the museum's Indonesian and Malaysian collections. This collection, comprised of over 1,500 objects that were collected between 1865 and 1910, were an unexplored part of the museum's material culture collection. Our investigation focused on the construction of various points of view, with the aim of finding alternative and experimental ways of exhibiting and presenting these ethnographic objects to the public.

Over a period of two years, we collaborated with a wide range of institutions, individuals, and communities: the MAXXI National Museum of Contemporary Art of Rome; Civico Zero, a centre for unaccompanied minor refugees; the Embassy of Indonesia; and a group of Indonesian students. Sometimes we took the opportuni-

---

5   The SWICH artist in residence, H. H. Lim, produced the third installation, *Origin of the Detail*, which examined the weapons of the museum's collections, connecting them with the process of artistic creation. The last installation focused on Elio Modigliani's collection and his book *A Journey to Nias* (1890), and included objects, notes from observations made in the field, archival materials, letters, and photographs on an ideal work table, which represented the creation process of the museographic exhibition itinerary. All the structures of the exhibition were realised by the self-funded social carpentry workshop K_ALMA, which trained roughly twenty asylum seekers and unemployed Italians.

ty presented by the project to deepen previous relations, as with MAXXI Museum and Civico Zero, both of whom we had started dialogue with two years before the beginning of SWICH Project.[6] In this case, the collaboration was the natural extension of past activities, mixing interpersonal and professional exchanges, and mutual participation in the other institutions' events, exhibitions, and programmes. We decided to involve MAXXI Museum for two reasons: as MAXXI is a contemporary art museum, partnering with them allowed us to feel more comfortable with the idea of hosting an artist-in-residence programme; and we shared general objectives in our desire to improve the social mission of our institutions, by organising audience-engagement programmes for young and migrant audiences. At the same time, CivicoZero asked to intensify our relationship and co-develop an educational programme, with the aim of integrating the activities of the museum with the programme of day-care facilities for unaccompanied children who make use of the centre. And, as the exhibition concept was about Indonesian collections, we decided, through the mediation of the Indonesian Embassy, to invite a group of Indonesian students to collaborate with us. Our aim was to involve difficult-to-reach audiences and give an educational perspective to the project.

Through a series of workshops, we developed a participative process with the aim of increasing the museum's ability to listen to and dialogue with these audiences, promoting the co-creation of heritage values, to generate new meanings for this heritage, by involving the audiences in museum content production, starting from the assumption that 'in its current meaning, heritage . . . is not just an asset with a value based on criteria of history and convention, but is a cultural product of enduring contemporary relevance' (Lattanzi 2012, 14). The idea was to give visitors an alternative tool to explore the museum's Indonesian and Malaysian collections. In particular, we decided to take a narrative approach, in order to promote new interpretations of the objects/artefacts, and to involve the so-called heritage communities, starting from their personal and cultural memories and then generating connections between participants and heritage.

### The Diaspora of Objects and People: Building a Plurality of Points of View on the Collections

A process to resignify the objects employed a narrative approach and the elicitation of audience-centred perspectives. We worked on the theme of 'diaspora objects' (Basu 2011), in an attempt to re-establish relations between objects and migrants while trying to recontextualise the collections within a global cultural landscape. Ethnographic ob-

---

6   This relationship started thanks to the parties' participation in a European project ('Brokering migrants' cultural participation' [https://mcpbroker.wordpress.com/]), where Stefania Vannini (MAXXI Public Engagement Department), Yves Legal (CivicoZero Centre), and Vito Lattanzi and Rosa Anna Di Lella (Pigorini Museum), along with other professionals in cultural and educational fields, participated in a series of seminars aimed at sharing experiences on migrants' participation in European cultural institutions.

jects take part in complex dynamics of representation of cultural belonging, where the museums, the territories of origin, and the communities of the diaspora all contribute to redefining the contemporary meaning of the objects preserved and exhibited in Western ethnographic museums. Thus, museum collections help in mediating the experiences of attachment and separation between 'living here' and the memory of other social contexts. Diaspora communities relate to their cultural histories in unpredictable ways, within social and economic contexts that generate both new meanings and values for objects and new forms of citizenship and belonging in migratory contexts.

Starting from this conceptual framework, the exhibition's intent was to enhance the mission of the ethnographic museum as a 'relational' entity, an institution called to take care not only of objects but also of relationships. This includes the museum's responsibility towards the communities whose history is interconnected with the collections stored in its depots. In line with this direction, the work was, above all, a reinterpretation of the objects beyond the classical interpretive grids of ethnographic museography.

We took as a starting point the idea that the meanings of objects are not established data, but rather they constantly evolve 'because they arise from a set of crossing viewpoints, from a game of mirrors that involved natives, missionaries, collectors, tourists and, later on, anthropologists' (Favole 2017, 109). They are always *plural objects*, both semantically and culturally, 'capable of activating the exchange and, at the same time, the negotiation of the meanings' (Favole 2017, 106). By involving people from various cultural backgrounds, we wanted to explore the 'density of objects' (Paini and Aria 2017), so as to explore the multiplication of cultural meanings of the objects themselves. Suspended between locations and belongings, the objects were placed under different lenses to unravel just how stratified and dense they can be. We intended the exhibition's installations to present a heritage *in diaspora* in transit between places and meanings, and *in dialogue* between narratives and voices of past and contemporary viewpoints.

## Diaspora Objects: Reconnections

The relation between museum and memory, identity and autobiography is at the core of the reflection on the museum and its renovation in the present. As Eileen Hooper-Greenhill (2007, 2) writes: 'museums are active in shaping knowledge: using their collections, they put together visual cultural narratives which produce views of the past and thus of the present'. Many ethnographic objects fit into the category defined by Janet Hoskins as 'biographical objects' (Hoskins 1998). These objects, often preserved in European museums, open up the possibility of creating new stories and interpretations within a renewed relationship between things and people, thus allowing access to forms of cultural intimacy in which heritage plays

Fig. 12.2. *Diaspora Objects: Reconnections.* In the museum's storage. Copyright: Museo delle Civiltà.

a key role in the forms of belonging and cultural representation (Dragojlovic 2016). In diaspora contexts, museum heritage can help communities to experiment with reconnecting with their personal and family memories, such as by reconstructing stories of migration and displacement. Autobiographical strategies, in particular, are increasingly used to involve audiences and construct deeper relationships between people and cultural heritage (Hill 2012; Clemente and Rossi 1999). In this way, heritage can be a catalyst for the renegotiation of identity and self-representation.

As many have pointed out, a wide range of activities and perspectives can be found under the umbrella of 'collaborative practices' (Clifford 1997, 1999; Karp, Kreamer, and Lavine 1991; Ames 1992; Phillips 2003; Golding and Modest 2013). In the framework of the SWICH collaborative exhibition, our intention was to go beyond forms of community consultation and participation that had already been experimented with in READ-ME projects. In order to expand the educational role of the museum and enlarge the range of the participatory practices beyond the main audience of our museum, we decided to engage young people with Indonesian cultural backgrounds and to ask them to co-create with us an installation, connecting with museum heritage through their own experiences and knowledge.

We realised that a participative process could forge reconnections between objects and people in the diaspora. The collaboration was oriented in two directions: first of all, to find an intimate and personal biography of the collections through the emotional resonance that the objects triggered in our young mediators; and second, to reactivate the dialogue between first- and second-generation migrants via the mediation of the objects stored in the museum. At the museum's Indonesian collection depot, the students selected objects as starting points to recount personal stories and experiences, connecting the museum's heritage to their life experiences and presenting some aspects related to the cultural contexts of origin. In addition, in order to better understand the cultural meaning of the objects, and improve connection with the Indonesian collections, we asked the students to do some research in the museum's library and to involve other members of their family.

Of the six students – Alessya, Anas, Isma, Evan, Viciana, and Vivaldi – only one had grown up in Rome; the rest were in Italy to attend university and would return to Indonesia once they completed their studies. The students entered into a relationship with the museum's objects in different ways, depending on their personal backgrounds, and each chose their object for emotional reasons. None expected to find Indonesian objects in Italy and they proudly considered them as cultural testimonies of their contexts of origin. As Evan said: 'Italy has an Indonesian cultural heritage that we ourselves do not necessarily have. . . . I am so proud to see it in other countries and I think this project can be further developed in the future'. Most of the students had a rather nostalgic attitude toward the objects, which reminded them of childhood experiences and a lost past. Vivaldi said, for example, 'I

Fig. 12.3. *Object in Transit: Transformations*. Mohamed H. and a photo-collage. Copyright: Museo delle Civiltà.

remember when I was a child staying at my grandmother's house on holiday. Her traditional Java home made me feel like I was living in the past'.

The collaboration with the six students was short in terms of duration but very productive in terms of outcomes. Texts, interviews, images, and items for the installation were produced by the students, both individually and in groups, during workshops held at the museum from May to December 2017. The result of this process of engagement was *Diaspora Objects: Reconnections*, a multivocal installation in which different visions intersected: the personal interpretation of the young mediators who presented their vision of the objects to the public through the mechanism of memory, the vision of other members of the Indonesian community involved by the mediators themselves, and, finally, the museographic description taken from the scientific literature.

## *Object in Transit: Transformations*

Another *engagement zone* (Onciul 2013) was created in the collaboration of young refugees (aged fourteen to eighteen) from the CivicoZero Centre with the MAXXI museum over more than two years (from the end of 2015 to the opening of the exhibition in February 2018). Onciul's expression 'engagement zone', which draws on James Clifford's (1999) theory of the museum as a contact zone, emphasises the cross-cultural relations and the dynamic, multiple dialogues in which participants engaged during the participative process.[7] The teenagers involved in the project were not a stable group, but rather constantly changed in number, cultural origin, interests, and attitudes, forming a movable, flexible, and unpredictable space of interaction.

In order to create an effective framework for this changing context, Pigorini museum's staff decided to guide the teenagers in a creative transformation of objects, with the aim of integrating the migration centre's educational activities with the museum's.[8] Throughout this process we found inspiration in the *Transformers*

---

[7] As Onciul (2013, 84) points out: 'The engagement zone is a physical and conceptual space in which participants interact. . . . It is a temporary, movable, flexible, living share of exchange that can occur spontaneously or be strategically planned. Engagement zones occur on frontiers, within groups, and as result of border crossings. They are semiprivate, semipublic spaces where on-stage and off-stage culture can be shared and discussed and knowledge can be interpreted and translated to enable understanding between those without the necessary cultural capital or to facilitate cross-cultural access'.

[8] The CivicoZero is a day centre located in the middle of Rome that provides support, guidance, and protection to migrant youngsters, aged between twelve and eighteen years of age, who find themselves in situations of social marginality, exploitation, and abuse. The centre is committed to improving their living conditions and protecting and promoting their rights. The supportive work is carried out by a multidisciplinary team who provide minors with the opportunity to express themselves in their own language, a requirement considered high priority, through several activities (photography, storytelling, tours in museums), in formal and informal contexts, including schools, museums, and theatres.

exhibition at the MAXXI Museum in Rome (11 November 2015 – 28 March 2016),[9] which allowed us to kick off a dialogue between a museum of contemporary art and an ethnographic museum. We focused our attention primarily on the work of Mexican artist Pedro Reyes, whose *Disarm* installation, which was created from scrap weapons collected and destroyed by the Mexican army, transforms guns and rifles into a mechanical orchestra. We organised a programme of workshops with the young refugees in collaboration with the MAXXI Public Engagement Office, including guided tours, storytelling activities, and photography workshops.

Because of difficulties in using verbal communication to create a space of mutual understanding, we decided to explore other languages, inviting them to access the Indonesian collections in a visual and creative way. They exchanged views with curators and artists, and created shared photo narrations of the MAXXI Museum and Pigorini Museum heritage. Using digital photography, the youths redesigned their personal relationship to the museum's spaces, creating a collective photo-map of their viewpoints and their impressions of the collections. The workshop led to the creation of three-dimensional collages, pieced together from the photographs taken during the various workshops. Thus, the teenagers transformed the museum's Indonesian and Malaysian objects, breaking them down and recomposing them according to their own perspectives. In the final installation, *Object in Transit: Transformations*, we presented the museum's objects as an educational tool, a means of socialisation and mediation, as well as a starting point for self-expression. The objects moved from one function to another, and they were represented, dissected, and regrouped according to a new way of seeing them. The images and the collages presented have become for us a representation of the experience of exploration and observation of the youngsters through a multiplicity of elements: from the rationalist geometries of the EUR, the neighbourhood in which the Pigorini Museum is located, to the details of the objects in the collections, from the MAXXI's contemporary art works to the objects in the Pigorini Museum's halls.

In this way, the process of involving young refugees of different origins and backgrounds created a more open setting for collaboration; the Indonesian objects were presented in a way that surpassed the issues of cultural belonging, as *objets prétextes* (Hainard and Kaehr 1984), for sharing a common path that goes beyond both the cultural contexts of the collections and the spoken languages and geographical origins of the participants. The objects became malleable and transformable, achieved through forms of collaboration between museums and people with experiences and stories of diversity.

---

9   The *Transformers* exhibition was curated by Hou Hanru and Anne Palopoli. More info at: https://www.maxxi.art/en/events/transformers/.

## The Participative Process: Questions and Issues

Collaborating allowed us to go beyond an 'object-oriented museology' (Brady 2009, 144-45), and to dispense with an essentialist notion of heritage, through which ethnographic museums have built their own representations and their theoretical paradigms over time, often giving unique and Eurocentric visions of the represented cultures. At the same time, these two engagement zones opened up a series of questions and issues; among them we would like to focus on the translation of the participative process into the design framework of the exhibition, and reflect on some crucial moments in the dialogue between the two curatorial teams.

### Sharing authority: A biographical approach

Including individual experiences is a way to share authority and acknowledge the authority of 'culture and experience' as being as important as 'scholarly authority', thus allowing for dialogue between distinct forms of expertise (Frisch 1990). As many have pointed out, the risk is to fix those involved in the role of either 'informant' or 'curator', or to hide the voice of either one, thereby reproducing hierarchical relationships in what is presented as a collaborative setting (Hutchison 2013, 145-46).

We decided to use a biographical approach in order to involve our audiences in the content creation process. This kind of approach was ultimately more effective, particularly as the expertise of the subjects involved was not strongly recognised – they are not expert in cultural heritage – and it also helped us in creating a comfort zone where the participants could feel at ease when asked to take on the role of the curator.

In our experience collaborating with the Indonesian students, some criticism emerged about the negotiation of the meaning of the objects selected. The non-coincidence between personal memories and the ethnographic meaning of the objects could have led to a conflict between the students' diasporic view and the experts' view on the objects. To avoid this risk, during the object selection phase, we let the students freely explore and share their personal memories, giving them more elements (books, articles, or other research materials) for cultural contextualisation. During the display design phase, we gave preference to the students' narratives, appending scholarly information as additional content that followed the first-hand accounts. In this way, the non-coincidence of the different interpretations was framed as an added value of the installation, conveying that the meaning of objects is not already given; it is obtained through processes that are constructed starting from the subjectivity of experiences.

### Exhibiting the process of collaboration

Another critical point, or rather unsolved issue, was how to represent the process of collaboration. This issue emerged strongly in the collaboration with young refugees, where in the final exhibition we wanted to communicate how the workshops' participants connected with the museum's collections. We felt that this was the project's most notable achievement.

But we found it difficult to give the public an idea of the complexity of the collaboration, to show the process through which the museum's objects were transformed and reshaped by the youths. We wanted to convey something about the participative process without exploiting the voices and the images of the teenagers, especially since they were 'unaccompanied minor refugees'. In other words, it was difficult to avoid giving a simplified, reconciled representation of the collaboration. This leaves unanswered questions such as: how can we display the outcomes of the participative process and the display-making process itself? Are audiences interested in the community engagement process when they visit an exhibition? How can we communicate the engagement process to the audiences in a way that avoids reducing the complexity and the polyvocality that may emerge during collaborative practices?

As Viv Golding (2013, 18) suggests, museums should 'become challenging museums, enriched by diverse perspectives, not silencing or avoiding difficult themes connected to various dilemmas'. Her words compel us to pay more attention to the way we plan, design, and produce an exhibition, especially when our objective is to experiment with process-oriented exhibitions focused on the 'making of' interpretations and viewpoints.

## What communities?

The exhibition, *The Making of a Point of View: Spotlights on the Indonesian and Malaysian Collections* tried to construct the meaning of the objects and implicitly build a sense of community in people's relationships with the museum space. This assumption raised some issues about museums' relationships with so-called communities in the larger Italian sociopolitical context.

In Italy, diaspora communities usually don't demand greater involvement or representation from museums. The Italian political and social context tend to frame 'the migration issue' under the category of 'emergency', with the risk of carrying out projects with a paternalistic perspective. This influences how museums interact with migrant communities: we host, give voice, empower, and share our authority by collaborating, engaging, and dialoguing with groups and individuals from outside the museum. This has crucial repercussions on the quality of the relationship between museums and diaspora communities, resulting in an unbalanced dialogue where only museum professionals shape the context of the encounter.

The experience of co-creation and collaboration carried out during the SWICH project has raised a crucial question: how can museums facilitate mutual understanding and social cohesion to rebalance the relationship with diaspora communities?

## Conclusions

*The Making of a Point of View* stimulated reflection on how polyvocality can be applied within and interact with the museum's curatorial procedures and rules. By focusing on the process of resignifying objects, we created a temporary contact-comfort zone with transcultural interpretive and curatorial teams, both composed of young participants working on two different installations of the SWICH project exhibition. Looking back on the participative process, it appears that co-creation practices can play a crucial part in reframing the role of the museum as a catalyst for social inclusion and cultural democratisation, and in fighting prejudices. In spite of all the difficulties and contradictions, collaborative practices can also help in developing more horizontal and pluralistic ways to represent cultures, going beyond hierarchical manners, opening up procedures of displaying objects, and bringing new values into the museum's public sphere.

## References

Ames, Michael. 1992. *Cannibal Tours and Glass Boxes: The Anthropology of Museums*. Vancouver: UBC Press.

Basu, Paul. 2011. 'Object Diasporas, Resourcing Communities: Sierra Leonean Collections in the Global Museumscape'. *Museum Anthropology* 34, no. 1: 28-42.

Brady, Miranda J. 2009. 'A Dialogic Response to the Problematized Past: The National Museum of the American Indian'. In *Contesting Knowledge: Museums and Indigenous Perspective*, edited by S. Sleeper-Smith, 133-155. Lincoln: University of Nebraska Press.

Clemente, Pietro, and Emanuela Rossi. 1999. *Il terzo principio della museografia*. Rome: Carocci.

Clifford, James. 1997. *Routes: Travel and Translation in the Late Twentieth Century*. Cambridge, MA: Harvard University Press.

Clifford, James. 1999. 'Museums as Contact Zones'. In *Representing the Nation. A Reader: Histories, Heritage and Museums,* edited by D. Boswell and J. Evans, 435-459. London: Routledge Press.

Dragojlovic, Ana. 2016. *Beyond Bali: Subaltern Citizens and Post-colonial Intimacy*. Amsterdam: Amsterdam University Press.

Favole, Adriano. 2017. 'Entangled Objects, Entangled People: etnografia di un oggetto condiviso'. In *La densità delle cose: Oggetti ambasciatori tra Oceania e Europa*, edited by A. Paini and M. Aria, 97-114. Pisa: Pacini.

Frisch, Michael. 1990. *A Shared Authority: Essay on the Craft and Meaning of Oral and Public History*. New York: State University of New York Press.

Golding, Viv. 2013. 'Collaborative Museums: Curators, Communities, Collections'. In *Museums and Communities: Curators, Collections and Collaboration*, edited by V. Golding and W. Modest, 13-31. London: Bloomsbury Academic.

Golding, Vivian, and Wayne Modest, eds. 2013. *Museums and Communities: Curators, Collections and Collaboration*. London and New York: Bloomsbury.

Hainard, Jacques, and Rolland Kaehr, eds. 1984. *Objets prétextes, objets manipulés*. Neuchatel: Musée d'ethographie de Neuchatel.

Hill, Kate, ed. 2012. *Museums and Biographies: Stories, Objects, Identities*. Woolbridge: Boydell Press.

Hooper-Greenhill, Eilean. 2007. *Museums and Education: Purpose, Pedagogy, Performance*. London: Routledge.

Hoskins, Janet. 1998. *Biographical Objects: How Things Tell the Stories of Peoples' Lives*. New York: Routledge.

Hutchison, Mary. 2013. '"Shared Authority": Collaboration, Curatorial Voice, and Exhibition Design in Canberra, Australia'. In *Museums and Communities: Curators, Collections and Collaboration*, edited by Viv Golding and Wayne Modest, 143-162. London: Bloomsbury Academic.

Iervolino, S. 2013. 'Museums, Migrant Communities, and Intercultural Dialogue in Italy'. In *Museums and Communities: Curators, Collections and Collaboration*, edited by Viv Golding and Wayne Modest, 113-129. London. Bloomsbury Academic.

Karp, Ivan, Christine Mullen Kreamer, and Steven D. Lavine, eds. 1991. *Museums and Communities: The Poetics and Politics of Museum Display*. Washington, DC: Smithsonian Institution Press.

Karp, Ivan, and Steven D. Lavine, eds. 1991. *Exhibiting Cultures: The Poetics and Politics of Museum Display*. Washington, DC: Smithsonian Institution Press.

Lattanzi, Vito. 2012. 'A Double-Gaze Museography'. In [S]*oggetti Migranti: dietro le cose le persone* [People behind the things], edited by K. Munapé, 11-19. Rome: Espera.

Lattanzi, Vito. 2014. 'The Pigorini Museum in Rome Facing Contemporaneity: A Democratic Perspective for Museums of Ethnography'. In *Advancing Museum Practices*, edited by Francesca Lanz and Elena Montanari, 73-82. Turin: Umberto Allemandi & Co.

Lattanzi, Vito, and Rosa Anna Di Lella. 2016. 'Al Museo con: patrimoni narranti per musei accoglienti'. In *Un patrimonio di storie: la narrazione nei musei, una risorsa per la cittadinanza culturale*, edited by S. Bodo, S. Mascheroni, and M. G. Panigada, 139-158. Milan: Mimesis Edizioni.

Onciul, Bryony. 2013. 'Community Engagement, Curatorial Practices, and Museum Ethos in Alberta, Canada'. In *Museums and Communities: Curators, Collections and Collaboration,* edited by V. Goldin and W. Modest, 79-97. London: Bloomsbury Academic.

Paini, Anna, and Matteo Aria. 2017. *La densità delle cose. Oggetti ambasciatori tra Oceania e Europa*. Pisa: Pacini Editore.

Phillips, Ruth. 2003. 'Community Collaboration in Exhibitions: Toward a Dialogic Paradigm'. In *Museums and Source Communities*, edited by L. Peers and A. K. Brown, 155-170. London: Routledge.

Sandell, Richard. 2002. 'Museums and the Combating of Social Inequality: Roles, Responsibilities, Resistance'. In *Museum, Society, Inequality,* edited by R. Sandell, 3-23. London: Routledge.

Fig. 13.1. *Fadi Haddad*. Photo by Aleksandra Pawloff for the exhibition *Out of the Box* at Weltmuseum Wien, Vienna.

# Out of Boxes: Touching wor(l)ds moving pictures

A Collective Case Study on a Collaborative Exhibition at the Weltmuseum Wien, Vienna.

UrbanNomadMixes

You can't go back and change the beginning but you can start where you are and change the ending.
- C.S. Lewis

## Context

How do we mobilise people from the Philippine community, indeed from any community, in Vienna to collaboratively develop an exhibition at the Weltmuseum Wien (WMW)? And how can objects from the museum's collections help in such community mobilisation? What role, for example, can a Catholic altar that the WMW acquired from a Filipina woman in Vienna before she left for the United States have in this collaborative work? Is the idea of a 'Filipino community' not already too closed, too restricted for any productive work? These were the questions that emerged for Camilo Antonio in early 2016, when he was asked to co-curate a WMW initiative to collaborate with communities in the city. Antonio had prior experience working with migrant communities in Vienna and was co-founder of the Club Filipino at the United Nations in Vienna. He was therefore familiar with community-based projects and welcomed such an invitation.

The theme that framed the project at the WMW, 'Connecting Diaspora Objects and Peoples', seemed to present great opportunities for connecting the museum's objects with community members. Camilo Antonio, however, found the focus on nationality too narrow an understanding of the theme. Through further discussions to find alternative approaches, the curatorial team decided to invite UrbanNomadMixes (UNM) to participate. UNM is a loose alliance, initiated by Antonio twenty years ago, of multinational performance artists and cultural activists who were known by and had worked with the museum.[1] In this short chapter, we present some brief reflections on the methodology developed for community involvement in the project. Coinciding with a growing interest among museums to

---

[1] UNMixers' collective biography: Our collective group of UrbanNomadMixers welcomed the challenge to write this article as a loose organic alliance of Vienna-based creative transcultural activists with a common history in making performative public interventions. Our diversity is reflected not only in the nationalities of our members but also in our work with artistic, academic, and nongovernmental associations with which we are able to proactively evolve partnerships for projects and event networks. Stephanie Misa, Franz Prüller, and Ruby Sircar initiated the idea for writing an article, which Antonina Boschitsch, Mae Cayir, Nael Elagabani, Kate and Pri Elamthuruthil, Vera Lacková, Itai Margula, Harold Otto, and Nadja Zerunian endorsed. Camilo Antonio conceptualized and redrafted the article in a group session that also included Neda Hosseinyar, Ramon and Marc Jarabe, Alina Șerban, and Inez Wijngaarde. Several more members have actively supported the effort prior to final editing by Antonio, Otto, and Prüller. As regards academic credentials, four among the group hold doctorates and the rest predominantly master's degrees; some are internationally recognized artists and/or are affiliated with the Academy of Fine Arts in Vienna.

work collaboratively with differently constituted communities, we hope that this essay will invite questions about what community work is or can be in museums.

## Framing Questions, or What Is Diaspora Anyway?

While the theme of the project, *connecting diasporas*, seemed self-evident, the mundane question of *what constitutes 'the diaspora' in objects and in people, and where are its physical or imaginary borders*? was one that had to be asked at the outset. It could not be assumed that the 'sacred' objects acquired by the WMW would correspond with participants' ideas of the 'sacred'. Diverse diasporic situations affect diaspora identities and practices in very different ways, and therefore it was important to think critically not just about the specific people who were involved in the project but also about which situations have what kind of effects on diaspora formations and therefore what narratives should be told in this project. Choosing members of UNM – 'UNMixers'- as the main protagonists was an attempt to address these complexities from the outset. Members wove their diverse and chosen stories – of movement, of memories of elsewhere, and of their current position in Vienna – into their narratives, which included, but were not limited to postcolonial narratives, and incorporated into these objects from the collections. 'Diaspora' in this project, then, was taken as practice, not as reducible identity. It describes states of mind that people, not limited to those with foreign or migrant backgrounds, mine through their imagination and their memories, and perform in relation to objects.

The need to establish the basic premises was raised by UNMixers at the outset. For example, Stephanie Misa questioned the relationship between UNM's manifesto and WMW's notion of community. Other members asked about how the institutional value of objects – ascribed to them by research processes, including categorization and labelling – affect those objects' symbolic meanings, which might be different from the meanings that community members may recognise. The writer Italo Calvino suggests that specific symbolic meanings are ascribed to objects when community members weave those objects into their narratives; such narratives then activate other meanings like a special force or pole in a magnetic field (Calvino 1996, 33).[2]

UNM's protagonists supported the orientation of their initiator, which emphasised that it was 'the mix' – an intersectional notion of identification – that promised non-reductive ideas about diaspora. This concept of the mix demands the resolution of tensions in identification, the straddling of a settled and unsettled urbanised existence, and the coming to terms with nomadic states of living that help

---

2  On ethnographic museums' perspectives and practices, we consulted sources including: Golding and Modest (2013); MacGregor (2012); and Kuhnt-Saptodewo et al. (2012).

us recuperate lost places or find 'elsewheres' that generate a rooted, and/or rerouted, sense of belonging. Such complex mixing can be found in narratives by UNMixers Neda Hosseinyar and Inez Wijngaarde, for example, as well as UNMixers who chose objects in pairs: siblings Antonina and Florian Boschitsch, father and son Ramon and Marc Jarabe, the couple Kate Elamthuruthil and Nael Elagabani, and the WMW co-curators themselves.[3] The diversity of UNMixers – Vienna-based multinational performance artists and creative transcultural activists – partnering with diverse 'insiders' in the museum, informs this process of diasporic 'mixing'.

This complex engagement with diaspora, mutually constituted through interaction, has been the guiding spirit of UNM that has been running through varied projects and events for over twenty years. This spirit finds expression in a 'manifesto', revised periodically, in much the same way UNM grows organically in membership and in its sense of community as it draws lessons from each project. The group's collective identity changes as its participants change over time. In this spirit, those who actively initiated and contributed to this project set out the following guiding concerns:

1. As settlers in Vienna who are guided by diasporic consciousness, we have been confronted by the urgent need to understand and address the eroding of the pluralistic model of societies in which we live. The ongoing tsunami of far-right political parties, populist voices, and neofascist nationalist movements in the European political landscape have questioned the constructive work that has been done over the last three decades to address the traumatic experiences of genocide and other hard lessons of Nazism and World War II.

2. As transcultural nomads, we have been empowered to value being a part of Austria, within whose supposedly pluralist structures and transparent social democratic processes we live and work.

3. As cultural activists, we believe in the proactive development of forms of co-existence by considering 'culture' in all its manifestations, not as fixed, canonical dogmas that divide, but as an epistemological, conceptual, and methodological tool for coming to terms with our current political arrangements.

4. As subjects/actors within society, we are guided by a shared value: that for cultural commitment to be meaningful, members of any society need the freedom to confront any problems, and the respect to be able to challenge sociohistorical structures that restrict their right to participate fully in society.

---

3  See section 'Diaspora Dialogues' in the catalogue for the *Out of the Box* exhibition (WMW 2018).

5. Our performative interventions are done to create 'spaces for confronting culture' which entails opening up 'internal borders of the mind', by which we can remember pasts while acting responsibly upon these memories in the present, whether through critical thought or through the imagination.

These are the concerns that animate our work as UNMixers – our manifesto – which we brought to the table in working with Weltmuseum Wien.

## Methodology, Structure, and Process

As protagonists in the project, UNMixers committed themselves to participate for more than a year in a series of intensive workshops that engaged with diaspora objects. This process produced displayable outcomes, including texts, video clips, and photographs. Interviews with UNMixers members involved a combination of qualitative social science techniques for generating oral history narratives.

The mix of products were put together in an audio-visual-graphic installation and in an exhibition catalogue. Importantly, the process required that the co-curators and the three commissioned artists (photographer Aleksandra Pawloff, videographer Marc Jarabe, and architect-designer Itai Margula) also involve themselves in the process, bringing the total of UNMixers to thirty participants. And, as the first of such collaborative projects in WMW's newly opened special exhibition area, *Out of the Box* included the museum's internal/external staff in various departments. Custodians opened up their collections as UNMixers researched and selected their objects from storage rooms in the WMW's basement. That process was, predictably, not always smooth sailing. As outsiders, UNMixers inevitably challenged WMW's institutional goals and framework. The tensions that emerged put the project to the test, especially because it involved an extended period of content generation on sensitive and substantive matters that showed differences in perceptions and values of the main protagonists on both sides, UNMixers and museum. Nevertheless, the project overwhelmingly resonated with diverse stakeholders, which could be seen in the positive support for the project, from testimonies on Instagram to requests for guided tours from external parties.

The idea of 'mirroring the diaspora effect' was the theme that unified a series of five workshops. This was complemented by a more complex methodological orientation devised by Camilo Antonio, which he describes as the 'poetics of diaspora effect': the push-and-pull of longing for the past and yearning for the future is a universal existential issue not limited to those who have left their original homes. It is a complex condition emanating from non-linear causal relations that arises from feelings of displacement and dispersion or loss of "home" and fragmentation or loss of self.[4] For Camilo Antonio, the point is that the project offered a platform to empower a community of UNMixers and to facilitate the WMW to go beyond the stereotypes of 'strange foreigners', 'diasporic terrorists', or 'unwanted migrants' (see Bauman 2015, 13). From a transcultural perspective, the project tried to shift the focus to something larger and deeper, rather than simply scapegoating migrants and refugees or globalisation. The problematic of the diaspora effect provides common ground to ask the crucial question: how do humans cope while in a state of being 'no-longer-there but not-yet-here'? The 'mix' in UNM cultural activism enables participants to courageously open up and push against reductive approaches to us vs them.

## Lessons Learned

How did the experience lead to better understandings of diasporic issues and practices, and how did that affect participants' perspectives? Preparing for and conducting the workshops empowered each object-subject 'mirroring' to think critically about diaspora effects. UNMixers were directly involved in offering critical observations on issues that affect them, including complex political-cultural currents and socioeconomic situations. They confronted systemic and institutional approaches to document, present, and archive objects, providing alternative ways of handling museum collections. A good amount of patience and flexibility were called for on both sides, and the crucial role played by museum counterparts Jani Kuhnt-Saptodewo and Doris Prlic, as they mediated between UNM and the museum, was a necessary one.

A sense of 'identity' or 'home' as an anchor of belonging and issues such as religion and ethnicity are the foci and cross-cutting threads which UNMixers use to engage – even therapeutically – the quest to find 'lost selves' or to journey to interior archives of one's own memories. In this process, memories of forgotten times and places were recovered and intimate healing stories were revealed. Several UNMixers reflected that, prompted by their chosen objects, they found it a revealing and cathartic experience to talk about their ties to origins, places, and memories as well as to people who have shaped their minds and ways of seeing the world. They mentioned that they realised that what people commonly call 'home' is not a place but people who make one feel accepted and at ease. Thus, despite 'not

---

4   This idea was developed in Antonio's doctoral dissertation, *Cultural Politics as Emancipatory Engagement through Heroic Poetics of Diaspora Effect* (University of Vienna 2017). In this work Antonio draws on the novels of the Philippine national hero José Rizal (written from the perspective of exile in Europe) along with the works of other scholars such as: John Docker's *1492: The Poetics of Diaspora* (2001); James Clifford and George Marcus' edited volume *Writing Culture: The Poetics and Politics of Ethnography* (1986); Paul Gilroy's *Small Acts: Thoughts on the Politics of Black Cultures* (1993); and the compendium book *Diasporas Reimagined*, edited by Nando Sigona et al. (2015).

yet being here', people can reach out from the security of these relationships to widen the circle of others with similar feelings.

The timescale of the project and dynamic engagement with the museum and each other took the UNMixers through a trajectory that enabled each one to rethink how to make each object come alive with footprints from diasporic reimaginings, which transported seemingly insignificant objects into the present. A small blue Madonna figurine with electrical wirings transported Alina Serban back to Romania, where she had seen such objects of protection in cars that became moving shrines; Vera Lacková reminisced about the Black Madonna, who is venerated by the Roma in southern France; there, her festive celebration as 'St. Sarah' also symbolises the Roma's discrimination as a people.

Identifying themselves as transcultural, UNMixers Pri Elamthuruthil and Ruby Sircar chose religious objects whose meanings were very personal to them, not taxonomical as they were in the museum. Stephanie Misa also made this point very clear in her choice, asserting that it's not the origin of tiny arrowheads (weapons that were cargo in the Spanish galleon trade between Acapulco, Mexico, and Manila two hundred years ago) that matters, nor is it how a German found them in the Philippines and brought them to Vienna. Rather, their significance for her is in confronting them at the WMW and the meanings they might hold for the future. In a seemingly comic vein, Harold Otto picked a souvenir object – an unidentifiable ceramic animal, presumably from an Amerindian tribe in Pueblo, New Mexico – from among the artefacts that Archduke Franz Ferdinand collected during an incognito trip to America.[5] Ingeniously, Otto traced his Alsatian ancestry from German migrants within the Old Order Amish and connected it to similarities with the Amish communities in Pennsylvania as cultures of resistance outside the mainstream United States.

In a way, 'our objects found us' is what Franz Prüller, Samira Rauter, Camilo Antonio, and Nadja Zerunian all claim. In the exhibition catalogue and video clips, they explain how tracing diasporic links with 'their objects' revealed new sources and meanings. The mask Prüller chose from Tierra del Fuego evoked *Ur Natur* and *Paradise Lost*; Rauter's 'model Iranian cradle' conjured the womb as the first home from which we humans are displaced, which held particular resonance as she learned she was pregnant during the project and her child was born right after the exhibition opened. Then there's the metaphor for transcultural diversity that Antonio saw in the soda pop tin cans brought back to Vienna from Asia by the artist Reinhold Mittersakschmöller, who then converted them into a prayer wheel. Upon seeing the colourful object leaning against the wall in a corner – instead of its usual horizontal position – Camilo Antonio saw it reflecting the group's dynamics while

---

5   These objects were part of the exhibition *Franz Is Here! Franz Ferdinand's Reise um die Erde*, curated by Christian Schicklgruber and Axel Steinmann at the WMW in 2014.

Fig. 13.2. *Camilo Antonio*. Photo by Aleksandra Pawloff for the exhibition *Out of the Box* at Weltmuseum Wien, Vienna.

also alluding to recycling and global flows. And with her choice of a nondescript tin can from Kurdistan, Nadja Zerunian sums up diasporic evocations in verse as her 'patina of memories' suggests: 're-purposed "kristal"/ supporting an ox./ resonance of movement/ promising escape' (WMW 2018).

Finally, looking at the project's outcomes in terms of metamorphosing images that are akin to emerging diasporic consciousness can lead to other diaspora effects: evoking a chain of imaginary events among the protagonists traversing landscapes of the mind. Considering the diasporic dialogues as going through a house of mirrors, we encounter alternative questions: Are you rooted 'Somewhere' or en route, in search of 'Anywhere'?[6]

## In Their Own Words

### Camilo Antonio

born in the philippines, my south pacific soul steers through an archipelago of islands, transacting cultural differences amid volcanic eruptions, stormy seas, and fault lines in mountains of memories that i mine while in the diaspora: reining in my sino-hispanic-malayan ancestry and spanish-american colonial history through studies in the colorado rockies and politicised washington, d.c. . . . having come to austria during the marcos dictatorship, i identify with people who take refuge from fatal insular games and power wars, . . . i concoct understandings of 'home' as a range of arrangements and anchors of belonging for rewiring minds in a vienna to return to. . .

urbannomadmixes parade in my mind when seeing multicoloured tin cans festooned and ready for a stomp, to be moved so as to free rhythmical music. . . resonances roll back to pop-up celebrations in southeast asia. . . children improvise fiestas banging cans and pots to create percussive excitement about comings-and-goings in provincial neighbourhoods becoming globally linked. . . in singapore a sling of singing soda pop cans trail behind cars of newlyweds leaving for honeymoons. . . in bhutan's temples painted metal and wood structures are strung as prayer mills: you touch one, you unleash chanting tones. . . atop himalayan hills prayer flags from pine poles flutter rainbow colours in the wind. . . dubai's skyscrapers echo. . . in vienna's stephansdom votive candles light up the cathedral. . . tourists' cellphones' clicking clicks crescendo. . .

---

6   See David Goodhart's interview: 'Eliten müssen Bescheidenheit lernen' in *Die Presse*, 6 May 2018. The editor of *Prospect* magazine and author of *The Road to Somewhere* (Oxford University Press, 2017) explains his thesis that values in today's globalised world divide people according to their socioeconomic goals into 80 per cent 'Somewheres' with the need to be rooted and 20 per cent 'Anywheres' who are at home in the world.

### Samira Rauter

My journey to Vienna began in Iran, where I was born in Tehran in the year of the Islamic Revolution.

As far back as I can remember, I have always been longing for a sense of being or feeling 'at home'. I do not feel that I belong to a specific nationality – neither the Austrian nor the Persian one. My identity is shaped by aspects of both cultures as well as by my childhood experiences with war and fleeing. I love living in this wonderful country of Austria. At the same time, however, I am also grateful for and value my roots that have taught me so much. I had the privilege of deciding for myself how I wanted to live as a woman in a modern European society and what role I wanted my faith to play in all that. At first I liked the cradle because of its symbolic value and the association with Iran as the 'cradle of humanity'. A little later, my Carinthian husband Hermann and I found out that we were expecting our first child. It was then that I became aware that I had probably chosen the cradle by intuition and for deeply personal reasons. Perhaps the objects actually find us and not the other way around. When I came into contact with the cradle itself, I experienced an even more intense connection to the object. People can decide to be free in their hearts and minds, even though they might feel trapped in conventional restraints. After all, the secret of freedom is courage.

### Fadi Haddad

It is possible that home is a place we've never been to. I grew up in Syria and have lived in Dubai, Singapore, Mexico City, and now Vienna. Wherever my parents are is where I feel at home. For five years now my parents have been living in Canada; and for five years I haven't been able to get a visa to visit my home there.

When I first saw this cookie cutter, it brought a smile to my face from ear to ear. I had flashbacks to my childhood in Syria: Mom baking, myself on the floor watching TV, our neighbours popping in spontaneously for a coffee and a chat. It was a wonderful home to grow up in. Contemplating the cookie shaper, I realised that this is the perfect representation of what Syria means to me. This cookie shaper doesn't make the cookie, it just makes it beautiful, gives it a shape and an identity. I've spent most of my adult life outside of Syria; today I live in Vienna. My friends are dispersed throughout the world, we communicate in English. I've travelled over forty countries and experienced the world. These are the ingredients that it takes to make my cookie, but being a Syrian is my only cookie shaper.

### Harold Otto

I've been in Vienna for more than a decade. I grew up bi-cultural: in the USA, but not of the USA. My 'non-American' family includes ancestors from, among other places, Alsace's Vosges Mountains. We belonged to a small ethnic-religious minority, the Amish, who regard obsessively ambitious, self-aggrandising values of the 'American Way of Life' a threat to their Christian identity.

I chose a nineteenth-century object from North America and from the Pueblo Cochiti culture that, like the Amish culture, quietly resists by withdrawing from the 'American Way of Life'. The Pueblo Cochiti people developed a complex civilisation that thrived in North America for centuries before Europeans encountered the continent. They, like the Amish, deliberately live according to spiritual values that seek to transcend the hegemonic culture. They are also in the USA, but not of the USA. This object does not come from the Pueblo Cochiti's traditional life and has no apparent significance for their spiritual practices. After transcontinental railroads infringed on the Pueblo lands, some used their traditional pottery skills to make ceramic 'stuff' that could be sold at train stops. Crown Prince Franz Ferdinand, during his world tour of 1893, stepped off his train distant from the Pueblo lands and purchased this figure (created for its portability and exotic appeal) at a market where traders sold a hodgepodge of 'Indian curios' to rich travellers.

The Old Order Amish and the Pueblo Cochiti are often 'exoticized' as somehow living an 'authentic' life. Both cultures follow peculiar rules that react against broader political-economic forces, sometimes simply to earn money by creating easily marketable handicrafts for outsiders. These mysteriously 'authentic' objects are suited for storage in a museum's archive to be puzzled over by future generations.

*These four contributions were previously published in the catalogue for the Out of the Box exhibition (WMW 2018, pp. 20, 21, 36, 37, 64, 65, 70, 71).*

## References

Bauman, Zygmunt. 2015. 'Diasporic Terrorism'. *IWMPost* 116: 13.
Calvino, Italo. 1996. *Six Memos for the Next Millennium.* London: Vintage.
Clifford, James, and George E. Marcus, eds. 1986. *Writing Culture: The Poetics and Politics of Ethnography.* Berkeley: Univ. of California Press.
Docker, John. 2001. *1492: The Poetics of Diaspora.* New York: Continuum Publishing Company.
Gilroy, Paul. 1993. *Small Acts: Thoughts on the Politics of Black Cultures.* New York: Serpents Tail.
Golding, Viv, and Wayne Modest, eds. 2013. *Museums and Communities: Curators, Collections and Collaboration.* London: Bloomsbury Publishing.
Kuhnt-Saptodewo, Sri, Ursula Brandl-Straka, Reinhard Maurer, and Thontji Taurissa, eds. 2012. *Maluku: Sharing Cultural Memory*. Vienna: Museum für Völkerkunde.

MacGregor, Neil. 2012. *A History of the World in 100 Objects*. London: Penguin Books and the British Museum.

Sigona, Nando, Alan Gamlen, Guilia Liberatore, and Hélène Neveu Kringelbach, eds. 2015. *Diasporas Reimagined: Spaces, Practices and Belonging*. Oxford: Oxford Diasporas Programme.

Weltmuseum Wien (WMW). 2018. *Out of the Box: Moving Worlds*. Exhibition catalogue. Vienna: Weltmuseum Wien.

Fig. 14.1. Exhibition view – *The future of the Slavery Past.* Afterlives of Slavery. Photo by Kirsten van Santen.

# For Contingent Collaboration: The Making of the *Afterlives of Slavery* Exhibition at the Tropenmuseum

RITA OUÉDRAOGO, ROBIN LELIJVELD, MARTIN BERGER, RICHARD KOFI, AND WAYNE MODEST

## Introduction

This chapter tells a story about the making of the *Afterlives of Slavery* exhibition, held in the Tropenmuseum, as a way of thinking through collaboration in museums. Taking representations of the slavery past as a starting point, we explore what is at stake in collaborative practices between stakeholders and museums, especially in relation to contested or controversial topics. We do not pretend this discussion is exhaustive, nor do we rehearse already existing scholarship on the theme; we are more interested in the horizon of possibilities that collaboration offers for thinking about more convivial futures.

## On Collaboration

'Collaboration' in Dutch is '*samenwerking*', from *samen* (together) and *werken* (to work). As a word, as a concept, it is as obvious as it is elusive. Hidden behind its' Latinate origins, 'collaborate' comes from the word *collaborare*, which means 'work with', from the prefix *com-* (with) + *laborare* (to work). The Cambridge English Dictionary defines collaboration as 'the situation of two or more people working together to create or achieve the same thing'[1]. In Dutch, *samenwerken*, the infinitive, and the noun form *samenwerking* do not pretend to hide their origins; their distinct compound parts make it clear: together and working. The Van Dale[2] dictionary defines '*samenwerken*' as working together in 'mutual consultation' (*in onderling overleg werken*). Both in English and in Dutch, the words seem to describe a similar act: labouring together toward shared ends. Yet in English there is another, more negative meaning: complicity. We need only to remember those who collaborated with the Nazis during WWII. Our intention in reminding the reader of these meanings is not to engage in wordplay but rather to invite the reader to think again about the complexity of what might be at stake in the idea of collaboration, especially within the context of museums and contested heritage.

The last few years have seen a growing interest in collaboration as an important part of the work of many museums, with ethnographic museums as key players in these developments.[3] With the professionalisation of the field, starting already in the 1970s and expanding in the 1980s, with the push for more inclusive practices, many museums made collaboration with diverse stakeholders a core part of their approach to issues of positionality, authority, voice, and perspectives.

---

1   *Cambridge English Dictionary*, s.v. '*Collaboration*'. Accessed 1 September 2018, https://dictionary.cambridge.org/dictionary/english/collaboration.
2   *Van Dale* Dutch dictionary, 'Samenwerking. Accessed 1, September 2018. https://www.vandale.nl/gratis-woordenboek/nederlands/betekenis/samenwerken#.XFDsOqHsY2w.
3   Much of this work goes back to the movement in museum studies called the New Museology (Vergo 1997). You should also see publications such as Peers and Brown (2003); Golding and Modest (2013); Watson (2007); and Karp, Kreamer, and Lavine (1992).

With this interest in collaboration, however, there has also been growing criticism. Proponents of collaboration suggest the practice promises an increased democratisation in terms of decision-making, and authority, and in the redrawing of the lines of power, but this promise is often not achieved in practice. Golding and Modest (2013), together with numerous scholars, have explored the potential of collaboration, as well as its limits, within the museum context.

## *Afterlives*: Towards 'Collaborative Curating'

Taking this criticism seriously, the Tropenmuseum embraced a collaborative approach to the development of the temporary exhibition *Afterlives of Slavery*. The starting point for this exhibition was the idea that we occupy a new moment, at least in the Netherlands, in researching, discussing, and representing the slavery past. *Afterlives* intervenes in these ongoing discussions regarding how to remember the slavery and colonial past in the present, and if and how this past continues to shape our present. It was, however, also an experimental exhibition, exploring what a collaborative approach might yield for rethinking the museum's practices in representing and addressing difficult histories. If in the past – and we have our doubts here – slavery was seen as a bygone era, an antiquarian interest for scholars and museum professionals to research, interpret, and represent as they wanted, if this was an internal debate among few scholars, the stakes have changed significantly in recent years. Indeed, it would not be an exaggeration to suggest, even if cynically, that the slavery past had become a site for competitive attention among cultural institutions, perhaps even among scholars, interested in scoring points for addressing it in the best way. And perhaps this is not a bad thing. If institutions and scholars are competing, their doing so suggests that the topic may have moved from the periphery to the centre of discussions of how certain histories, and the slavery past in particular, shape our present, and what we should do with this past.

Historians and institutions should, however, not be the only ones credited or blamed for this shift, even if they play an important role. This shift also signals the importance of grassroots and not-so-grassroots activism, along with other popular demands for alternative forms of historiography, that have worked to redistribute the power to define how the slavery past should be represented in the present (see Trouillot 1996).

It is with these shifts in mind that the Tropenmuseum 'collaboratively curated' *Afterlives*, realising that addressing such topics must be done together with others, especially with those who feel most directly the impact of colonialism's effects in the present.

## Creating *Afterlives*

From the outset, the museum realised that the theme of the exhibition was one that had become a 'hot topic' (Cameron and Kelly 2010) that many fear threatens to polarise Dutch society. Slavery is not just a historical topic, but one that has shaped the Netherlands as it is today; it is part of the personal heritage and lived reality for many in Dutch society. We knew that the museum's voice was only one of many in the debate, and we wanted to move away from the idea of the museum as an institution that creates 'the definitive narrative' on the Dutch colonial past and its material culture. It was also an attempt to move away from popular ways of narrating Dutch history, which understood the slavery past as a dark page in an otherwise Golden Age.

The exhibition had a traditional core exhibition team, including a curator, an exhibition maker (interpreter), and a supporting researcher/curator. This team was complemented by a standing advisory committee that guided the curators in selecting objects, defining the narrative that the exhibition would tell, and writing display texts. This committee included academics, activists, and heritage specialists, chosen intersectionally across forms of identification including ethnicity/'race', gender, and age. Curatorial meetings were organised throughout the process around different aspects of the exhibition. This method of exhibition making was not simply about multivocality, a concept that is both difficult to define and to put into practice, but also an attempt to decentre museum as an authority.

The Tropenmuseum has a long history of curating exhibitions that engage with the Dutch colonial past and its afterlives, exhibitions that themselves have been criticised. Different from other recent exhibitions in the Netherlands,[4] however, one of our guiding principles for the exhibition was that it would not be a chronological presentation of a set of dates and facts, but rather an exploration of the contemporary legacies of the slavery past, articulated through a set of themes and narrated by key figures. It would be a history of the present, explored in themes such as: (Un)freedom, Creativity/Resilience, and the Creation of Race and Resistance. Traditionally, museum professionals have controlled the creation of meaning around objects in their collections. Often, at least in the Netherlands, the idea of 'neutrality' was central to exhibitions and exhibition texts, as the museum was not seen as a political actor, but rather as an archive for cataloguing sociocultural developments and trends. However, this supposed neutrality many times unconsciously reproduced white, cisgender, Eurocentric perspectives. In the *Afterlives* exhibition we aimed to move away from this false idea of neutrality and actively chose to (at least to attempt to) take the perspective of the enslaved and their descendants as a starting point. We wanted to look for counter-perspectives to mainstream histories, and

---

4   While different from *Afterlives*, the Tropenmuseum staged the exhibition *Black and White* in 2013, which was also more concerned to present slavery not as a finished past, but as past that still had its impact on Dutch society.

to approach the complexities of transatlantic slavery, colonialism, and contemporary racism in a human and humane way.

The only way to achieve this was by working together with others outside of the museum. We found this especially important as two of the three curators of the exhibition were white and none of the curators had a Dutch Caribbean or Indonesian background. This approach forced us to continuously question our own preconceived ideas and prejudices and opened our eyes to many mistakes and oversights. For example, in a text on Buki, a Maroon fortress, we said that the fortress was difficult to conquer and get under Dutch colonial control. One of our advisors, Aspha Bijnaar, reminded us that if we truly wanted to write from the perspective of the (formerly) enslaved, we should rephrase the text to say that the fortress was valiantly defended and only fell to the Dutch after a long siege. In the later stages of the project, advisors from the group Decolonize the Museum reviewed all the exhibition texts for similar mistakes and oversights. We hoped that through this process, through this intense collaboration, we could achieve a different kind of telling of the slavery past and its afterlives in the present.

## Collaboration, Power, and Contingency

Can collaboration be more than a promise? Is it a hope of doing things together and of doing them otherwise, but a hope that cannot be fulfilled? These questions informed the project to create *Afterlives*. Scholars and practitioners alike increasingly view collaboration as an important strategy for sharing power. However, they also acknowledge that much of the dispute about collaboration emerges exactly because of unfulfilled promises. Richard Sennett (2012, 5) has argued that the act of cooperating, of collaborating, is wrapped in the 'belief of mutual pleasure', which requires of 'people the skill of understanding and responding to one another in order to act together'. Underpinning such a claim – the claim to mutuality and pleasure, understanding and responding – is the possibility of a kind of equality. Yet Sennett does not ignore the difficulties of realising such aspirations. Indeed, he goes on to state that collaboration is also 'full of difficulty and ambiguity and often lead[s] to destructive consequences' (Sennett 2012, 5) . Equality and mutuality, then, are the horizon of hope that collaboration promises.

Writing about collaboration as a practice, especially when the political stakes in the shared work are high, Eve Tuck and K. Wayne Yang (2012) advocate for contingent collaborations over the false promise of solidarity. Working with contingency acknowledges the fact that while one may hope to redraw the boundaries of power, in practice productive and transformative collaborations take shape in the relations across power; in fact this is where they can be most fruitful. Here, contingency means acknowledging the different aims and desires of the collaborating partners, and working through these differences to achieve a common end.

Fig. 14.2. Exhibition view – *What is the price of freedom?*. Afterlives of Slavery. Photo by Kirsten van Santen.

Being transparent about common goals, about the nature of the collaboration, and about what each party wants to get from the project is important (see also Tuck and McKenzie 2015). Writing on collaboration in museums, Nancy Mithlo (2004, 74) describes this as the unmasking of underlying inequalities, through which appropriations and prejudices can be overcome. It is this form of contingent collaboration that we wanted to achieve in *Afterlives*.

## Listening and Learning Together, or Collaboration as a Future Practice

This chapter is a reflection on both the process of creating *Afterlives* and the collaboration that created it. The partners with whom we worked to create the exhibition were invited to criticise the process as well as the results, and we published their essays in a 'zine' as a legacy of the process. We invited them to write freely and openly about their experiences, acknowledging, as social anthropologist Ivan Karp (in Silverman 2015; see also Ferracuti, this volume) suggests, that 'collaboration is an opportunity to fail in the most splendid way'. It was not our intention to intervene, to edit the content of their articles or their ideas. We wanted them to explore whether the end results of the process were different from what they had hoped. What was it like working together within institutional limits? Did they stand by the project's outcome? And how could we improve our collaboration as practice?

Our collaborators brought different expertise to the table. They brought personal, professional, and institutional experiences with them, from which we benefitted. Together, this formed part of the museum's new way of working, in which we foreground critical listening and collaborative learning as important practices to push a more inclusive agenda. Indeed, a significant part of the critique of our kind of museums, ethnographic or world cultures museums, in the past was that we were too busy telling, putting our narrative out there, ignoring other voices. This is surprising, given the fact that listening is one of the central methodologies of the discipline with which we have shared a long history, that of anthropology.

The question that we now ask is: what does it mean to listen to activists, to members of diverse communities, to academics, and to the public, alike? What does it mean to listen, when what is being said is critical of the work you do? Producing *Afterlives* and the zine was an act of critical listening, one that brought diverse, even dissonant voices together so that we could learn, together, how to develop more inclusive practices.

This form of listening is not passive, but informed by an idea of collaboration as complicity, as collusion, in Sennett's words. And here we do not mean complicity in a negative sense. Rather we see it as taking common responsibility for a better future. If anything else, the *Afterlives* exhibition, as an experiment in the art of collaboration, was part of a commitment to a process that was, in fact still is,

Fig. 14.3. Exhibition view – *visitor filling in comment card.* Afterlives of Slavery. Photo by Kirsten van Santen.

full of difficulty and ambiguity. The consequences were, however, not destructive; they continue to inform our effort to gain awareness of how the colonial past has shaped and continues to shape our present, and to guide our ongoing inquiry into how we can help create more inclusive futures.

## Collaboration Towards Healing

The opening of the exhibition was not the end of the project. Indeed, the museum considers its visitors one of the main stakeholders with whom we collaborate. Within the centre of the exhibition we designed a space for participation, where visitors can leave comments and respond to a set of questions that relate to the guiding themes of the exhibition: (un)freedom, (in)humanity, refusal, and resilience. On a daily basis and in plentiful amounts, visitors write comments and reflections on blank cards that are then hung upon the gridded structure of the exhibition design. Slowly the responses form a temporary body of visitors' expressions, of hope and despair, shame and pride, innocence and guilt, regret and mercy, joy and fear, anger and delight, relief and discomfort, distrust and trust. This papered grid has become a site for encounter, in person and through writing, as visitors respond to each other's text.

Working with these comment cards is anything but new as a museological approach to engage with the public, whoever they might be. Most museums use them to collect feedback, and this is no different in our case. However, this feedback will inform our preparation for a new semi-permanent gallery on slavery and colonialism in 2021. We remove the cards periodically and document them. But this rather time-consuming process is not the challenge that we face; it is the issue of complicity that we continuously struggle with. Are we – in a serious attempt to decolonise the institution and its practices – truly decentring our authority as an ethnographic museum when we invite (or is it: 'allow') visitors to participate? If we were to think of the museum's responsibility for doing justice to those whose (hi)stories were once denied, can participation or collaboration work in processes of healing? Answers to these questions are not easy. We however believe that a horizon of justice can only be sketched by taking our stakeholders seriously, especially those to whom we have failed to listen in the past.

Now that the exhibition has been open for over a year, we continue to have regular conversations with outsiders about its content. Dutch police commissioners have visited the exhibition to consider how they can further discussions on racism and discrimination in their ranks, students have shared their critiques and comments, activists and academics have suggested improvements and changes. Our hope is that *Afterlives of Slavery* will remain a work in progress, serving as a source for discussion and an arena for debate in the years to come.

*Note: An earlier version of this text was published in the zine: Co-lab, published by the Research Center for Material Culture, as part of the Sharing a World of Inclusion Creativity and Heritage (SWICH) project.*

## References

Cameron, Fiona, and Lynda Kelly, eds. 2010. *Hot Topics, Public Culture, Museums*. New Castle upon Tyne: Cambridge Scholars.

Golding, Viv, and Wayne Modest, eds. 2013. *Museums and Communities: Curators, Collections and Collaboration*. London and New York: Bloomsbury Academic.

Karp, Ivan, Christine Mullen Kreamer, and Steven Lavine, eds. 1992. *Museums and Communities: The Politics of Public Culture*. Washington, DC: Smithsonian Publishers.

Mithlo, Nancy Marie. 2004. '"Red Man's Burden": The Politics of Inclusion in Museum Settings'. *The American Indian Quarterly* 28, no. 3-4: 74.

Peers, Laura, and Alison K. Brown. 2003. *Museums and Source Communities: A Routledge Reader*. London: Routledge.

Sennett, Richard. 2012. *Together: The Rituals, Pleasure and Politics of Cooperation*. New Haven: Yale University Press.

Silverman, Raymond A. 2015. 'Introduction: Museum as Process'. In *Museum as Process: Translating Local and Global Knowledges*, edited by Raymond Silverman, 1-18. New York: Routledge.

Trouillot, Michel-Rolph. 1996. *Silencing the Past: Power and the Production of History*. Boston: Beacon Press.

Tuck, Eve, and Marcia McKenzie. 2015. *Place in Research: Theory, Methodology, and Methods*. New York: Routledge.

Tuck, Eve, and K. Wayne Yang. 2012. 'Decolonization Is Not a Metaphor'. *Decolonization: Indigeneity, Education & Society* 1, no. 1: 1-40.

Vergo, Peter, ed. 1997. *New Museology*. London: Reaktion Books.

Watson, Sheila, ed. 2007. *Museums and Their Communities*. New York: Routledge.

# Biographies of Contributors

### Claudia Augustat
Claudia Augustat studied ethnology at the University of Bonn and was awarded her PhD from the Goethe University in Frankfurt am Main. She worked at the Weltkulturen Museum in Frankfurt and at the Ethnological Museum in Berlin before she became the curator for South American Collections at the Weltmuseum Wien in 2004. From 2015 to 2017 she was curatorial project manager for the refurbishment of the Weltmusuem Wien and in January 2018 she became project leader of the EU-funded SWICH project. Her research focuses on Amazonian collections from the nineteenth century, material culture and cultural memory, collaborative curatorship and the decolonisation of museum practice.

### Bianca Baldi
In her films, installations, photographs and images, Bianca Baldi addresses hidden infrastructures and narratives of power. Evoking the histories of film, studio photography and Trompe-l'œil, she positions carefully chosen objects and images revealing complex webs of political, economic and cultural influences. Born in Johannesburg, South Africa, Baldi obtained a Bachelor of Arts in 2007 from the Michaelis School of Fine Art (Cape Town, South Africa) and completed her studies at the Städelschule (Frankfurt, Germany). Her work has been featured in large international exhibitions such as the 11th Rencontres de Bamako (Mali), the 11th Shanghai Biennale (China), the 8th Berlin Biennale (Germany) and group exhibitions at Kunsthalle Bern (Switzerland), Extra City Kunsthal (Antwerp, Belgium), Kunstverein Braunschweig and Kunstverein Frankfurt (Germany). Recent solo exhibitions include 'Versipellis' at Superdeals, Brussels (Belgium), 'Eyes in the Back of Your Head' at Kunstverein Harburger Bahnhof (Germany), and 'Pure Breaths' at Swimming Pool, Sofia (Bulgaria).

### Martin Berger
Martin Berger holds a PhD in Archaeology from the University of Leiden. He is the curator for Central and South America for the Tropenmuseum, Museum Volkenkunde and the Africa Museum in the Netherlands. He has curated several exhibitions and was co-curator of the *Afterlives of Slavery* exhibition at the Tropenmuseum.

## Rosa Anna Di Lella
Rosa Anna Di Lella was trained as an anthropologist and is a member of the research staff of the 'Istituto Centrale per la Demoetnoantropologia' (Central Institut for Demo-ethno-anthropology, Ministry of Cultural Heritage and Activities and Tourism). She is also curator of the collections of the former Italian Colonial Museum at the Ethnographic Division of the Museo delle Civiltà. Di Lella has worked on a number of museological projects with migrant communities, together with public and private institutions.

## Sandra Ferracuti
Sandra Ferracuti holds a PhD in Cultural Anthropology (Università 'Sapienza' di Roma, 2008) and is currently curator for the Africa collections at the Linden-Museum Stuttgart (Germany). From 2010 to 2016 she was Adjunct Professor at the Università degli Studi della Basilicata (Matera, Italy), where she taught Museum Studies, Cultural Anthropology, and Anthropology of Cultural Heritages. She was Research Fellow at the same University from 2012 to 2014, working on a research project that investigated the protagonists, characters, and movements of Basilicata´s contemporary "heritage communities". Since 2002 she has been co-editor of the journal *Antropologia Museale* [Museum anthropology] and in 2014 she also became a member of the editorial board of *Archivio di Etnografia* [Ethnography archives]. From 2009 to 2013, she was Research Assistant at the Ethnography Division of the Museo Nazionale Presitorico Etnografico 'Luigi Pigorini' in Rome, where she supported the museum in its participation in the European Project RIME, Ethnography Museums and World Cultures. Ferracuti has conducted long-term ethnographic research in Italy and Mozambique. Her current research focuses on 'heritage frictions' between Africa and Europe and issues of citizenship in Europe, from the analytical perspective of the anthropology of museums, heritage, and the arts.

## Salvador García Arnillas
Salvador García Arnillas holds a PhD in Philosophy from Comillas Pontifical University and a master's degree in Art History from Autonomus University of Madrid. He is Curator at the Ethnological and World Cultures Museum (Barcelona), professor of Aesthetics at Ramon Llull University and invited professor of Museology at Saint Pacian University Athenaeum.

## Jacqueline Hoàng Nguyễn
Jacqueline Hoàng Nguyễn is an artist using archives and a broad range of media to investigate issues of historicity, collectivity, utopian politics and multiculturalism via feminist theories. She is currently a PhD candidate in the 'Art, Technology and Design' program at Konstfack – University of Arts, Crafts and Design and KTH Royal Institute of Technology. Nguyễn completed the Whitney Independent Study

Program, New York, in 2011, having obtained her MFA and a post-graduate diploma in Critical Studies from the Malmö Art Academy, Sweden, in 2005, and a BFA from Concordia University, Montreal, in 2003. Born in Côte-des-Neiges, she is currently based in Stockholm..

## Alana Jelinek

Alana Jelinek is a practising artist, exhibiting nationally and internationally for over 25 years. She works in a wide range of media, including participatory, film, sound, novel-writing and painting. From 2009 until 2017 she worked with the Museum of Archaeology and Anthropology, University of Cambridge, first as Arts and Humanities Research Fellow (2009-2014) and then as Senior Researcher for Pacific Presences (2013-2018), making site-specific work and responding to the collections and their histories in order to explore legacies of colonialism. Jalinek has written on art for the *Journal of Social Anthropology*, *Ethnos* and the *International Encyclopedia of Anthropology*. She is also the author of the monograph *This is Not Art* (2013), which theorises the discipline of art from the perspective her years of working with the Museum. She is currently Fellow of Art and Public Engagement at the University of Hertfordshire.

## Rajkamal Kahlon

Rajkamal Kahlon is a Berlin-based American artist and educator. Kahlon's archive-based painting practice addresses the overlap between colonial visual legacies and intimate forms of trauma. She creates symbolic spaces of visual rehabilitation for those that can no longer speak – the disappeared, the silenced and the erased. Kahlon received her MFA from the California College of Art and is an alumna of the Whitney Independent Study Program.

## Richard Kofi

Richard Kofi is an exhibition maker (interpreter) at the Tropenmuseum, Museum Volkenkunde, and the Africa Museum, in the Netherlands. He co-curated the *Afterlives of Slavery* exhibition at the Tropenmuseum, and the *Carnival Worldwide* exhibition at the Africa Museum. Both exhibitions foreground Kofi's interest in exploring alternative perspectives on mainstream historical narratives. Richard Kofi holds a master's degree in Cultural Studies from the Radboud University, Nijmegen. He is also a practicing artist.

## Robin Lelijveld

Robin Lelijveld holds degrees in Art History and Curatorial Studies and is a researcher at the Research Center for Material Culture (Tropenmuseum, Museum Volkenkunde, Africa Museum and Wereldmuseum). Her research interests include the visual and material culture of transatlantic slavery and the Dutch empire. She was one of the editors for the professional publication *Words Matter: An Unfinished Guide to Word Choices in the Cultural Sector*. Lelijveld was part of the curatorial team of the *Afterlives of Slavery* exhibition at the Tropenmuseum.

## Wayne Modest

Wayne Modest is the Head of the Research Center for Material Culture, the research institute of the Tropenmuseum, Museum Volkenkunde, Africa Museum and Wereldmuseum in the Netherlands. He is also Professor of Material Culture and Critical Heritage Studies in the Faculty of Humanities at the Vrije Universiteit Amsterdam. Modest was previously head of the curatorial department at the Tropenmuseum, Amsterdam; Keeper of Anthropology at the Horniman Museum in London; and Director of the Museums of History and Ethnography in Kingston, Jamaica. He has published widely on issues of belonging and displacement; histories of (ethnographic) collecting and exhibitionary practices; and difficult/contested heritage with a special focus on slavery, colonialism and post-colonialism. His most recent publications include *Victorian Jamaica* (Duke University Press, 2018, with Tim Barringer), and 'Anxious Politics in Postcolonial Europe' (*American Anthropologist*, 2017, with Anouk de Koning).

## Rita Ouédraogo

Rita Ouédraogo is the Research Programmer and (Community) Collaborations officer at the Research Center for Material Culture. Ouédraogo has worked on several community-based projects centred around museum collections. Informed by her ongoing research into questions of *Samenwerking* and *Solidariteit* (collaboration and solidarity), her work explores modes of collaborative practices across power differentials, especially within a decolonial framework. Ouédraogo holds a master's degree in Anthropology.

## Loretta Paderni

Loretta Paderni is an ethnologist, coordinator of the Museo Nazionale Preistorico Etnografico 'Luigi Pigorini' and director of the Asia department of the same museum. Her main research interests include the study and enhancement of collections, and of the documentary, archival and photographic heritage of the museum. Paderni has published numerous articles and essays around these themes, and organized and coordinated several exhibitions. Since 2007 she has been engaged in European projects focused on redefining the place and role of ethnography museums in several European countries. She is also part of the team developing definitions of systems for cataloguing material and immaterial heritage with the Central Institute for Cataloguing and Documentation.

## Tina Palaić

Tina Palaić is cultural anthropologist and pedagogue. Her professional career started in the Slovenian School Museum. Since 2013, she has collaborated with the Slovene

Ethnographic Museum as curator and educator. Her research interest focuses on museology innovation and the inclusive practices for under-represented voices.

## Aleksandra Pawloff

Aleksandra Pawloff is a freelance photographer based in Vienna, Austria. She describes herself as a 'people photographer', highlighting the emphasis in her work. Pawloff has travelled extensively for work, especially across Africa. She is currently working on a series of exhibitions on the theme of migration and home.

## Laura Peers

From 1998 until 2018, Dr Laura Peers was Curator for the Americas Collections, Pitt Rivers Museum, and Professor of Museum Anthropology at the University of Oxford. Trained both as an historian and an anthropologist, her work has explored the meanings of heritage objects to Indigenous people today in healing from colonial oppression and the shifting nature of relationships between museums and Indigenous peoples. She is now Adjunct Professor in the Department of Anthropology at Trent University, Canada.

## Barbara Plankensteiner

Barbara Plankensteiner is Director of the Museum am Rothenbaum World Cultures and Arts (MARKK) in Hamburg, Germany. She formerly worked as senior curator for African Art at the Yale University Art Gallery, and as deputy director, chief curator, and curator of the Africa Collection at the Weltmuseum Wien. She has published widely on the history of ethnographic museums and collecting, African art, and material culture.

## Doris Prlić

Doris Prlić was coordinator of the European cooperation project SWICH (Sharing a World of Inclusion, Creativity and Heritage) at Weltmuseum Wien from 2015 to 2018. She previously worked as an independent curator, realizing projects for different cultural organisations such as Festival der Regionen or afo (architekturforum oberösterreich, Linz, Austria). Prlić was one of the co-curators of the exhibition *Out of the Box* at Weltmuseum Wien. She holds a master's degree in Arts and Culture (track: Artistic Research) from the University of Amsterdam and a degree in Fine Arts from Art University Linz.

## Lluís-Josep Ramoneda Aiguadé

Lluís-Josep Ramoneda Aiguadé is Head of Collections at the Ethnological and World Cultures Museum (Barcelona). Between 2000 and 2016 he worked on several documentation projects for contemporary collections at the Museums of Barcelona. His research interests include the use of oral sources in collections-based research.

## Bojana Rogelj Škafar

Bojana Rogelj Škafar is an ethnologist and art historian with a PhD in sociology. She has worked for the Slovene Ethnographic Museum since 1989, where she was director from 2005 to 2015. Since 2015 she has resumed her curatorial career. Her research interests include Slovene folk art collections, the interpretation of pictorial sources for the purposes of ethnological research, visual culture studies and the history of SEM. She has published extensively in these areas.

## Nicholas Thomas

Nicholas Thomas has been the director of the Museum of Archaeology and Anthropology in Cambridge since 2006. He has written extensively on cross-cultural encounters as well as on empire and art in the Pacific. His list of publications includes *Entangled Objects* (1991), which was highly influential in the revival of material culture studies; *Islanders: The Pacific in the Age of Empire* (2010), for which he received the Wolfson History Prize; and *The Return of Curiosity: What Museums are Good for in the 21st Century* (2016). Thomas has curated numerous exhibitions, several in collaboration with artists, in Australia, New Zealand, and the United Kingdom, including 'Oceania' for the Royal Academy of Arts in London and the musée du quai Branly – Jacques Chirac in Paris.

## UrbanNomadMixes

UrbanNomadMixes is an organic alliance of Vienna-based creative transcultural activists with a common history in making performative public interventions. The group's members are characterized by diversity that is not solely reflected in the nationalities of the members but also in them belonging to different artist, academic and non-governmental associations. Stephanie Misa, Franz Prüller, and Ruby Sircar initiated the idea for writing an article, which Antonina Boschitsch, Mae Cayir, Nael Elagabani, Kate and Pri Elamthuruthil, Vera Lacková, Itai Margula, Harold Otto, and Nadja Zerunian endorsed. Camilo Antonio conceptualized and redrafted the article in a group session that also included Neda Hosseinyar, Ramon and Marc Jarabe, Alina Serban, and Inez Wijngaarde. Several more members have actively supported the effort prior to final editing by Antonio, Otto, and Prüller. As regards academic credentials, four among the group hold doctorates and the rest predominantly master's degrees; some are internationally recognized artists and/or are affiliated with the Academy of Fine Arts in Vienna.

This book is published in the frame of the project SWICH – Sharing a World of Inclusion, Creativity and Heritage. Ethnography, Museums World Culture and New Citizenship in Europe.

Co-funded by the Creative Europe Programme of the European Union.

The European Commission support for the production of this publication does not constitute an endorsement of the contents which reflects the views only of the authors, and the Commission cannot be held responsible for any use which may be made of the information contained therein.

---

SWICH, Sharing a World of Inclusion, Creativity and Heritage, was a four-year collaborative project among ten European museums, together with diverse stakeholders. The project was aimed at developing new strategies for future-oriented ethnographic museum practice. Between October 2014 and September 2018 partner museums produced a series of conferences, workshops, publications and collaborative exhibitions and worked collaboratively with artist and stakeholder communities to address some of the central issues facing ethnographic museums today in relation to Europe's colonial past, and its postcolonial (post)migrant present.

SWICH Project Partners
Weltmuseum Wien (KHM-Museumsverband), Vienna, Austria, Lead Partner
National Museum of World Cultures, Leiden/Amsterdam/Berg en Dal, Netherlands
Royal Museum for Central Africa, Tervuren, Belgium
Mucem – Museum of European and Mediterranean Civilisations, Marseille, France
National Museums of World Culture, Stockholm/Gothenburg, Sweden
Linden-Museum Stuttgart, Germany
Museo delle Civiltà/Museo Preistorico Etnografico 'Luigi Pigorini', Rome, Italy
Museum of Archaeology and Anthropology, Cambridge, United Kingdom
Slovene Ethnographic Museum, Ljubljana, Slovenia
Barcelona Ethnological and World Cultures Museum, Spain
Culture Lab, Tervuren, Belgium